Simply This

Simply This

PRINTED AND DYED
HANDMADE PROJECTS

FIONA FAGAN

NEW
HOLLAND

To Ella and Tess

First published in 2013 by
New Holland Publishers Pty Ltd
London · Cape Town · Sydney · Auckland

Garfield House 86–88 Edgware Road
London W2 2EA United Kingdom

Wembley Square First Floor Solan Road
Gardens Cape Town 8001 South Africa

1/66 Gibbes Street Chatswood NSW 2067 Australia

218 Lake Road Northcote Auckland New Zealand

www.newhollandpublishers.com

A record of this book is held at the British Library and the National
Library of Australia

ISBN 978 1 74257 435 6

Managing director: Fiona Schultz
Publisher: Lliane Clarke
Designer: Tracy Loughlin
Editor: Simona Hill
Proofreader: Nicole McKenzie
Photographs: Sue Stubbs and Fiona Fagan
Production director: Olga Dementiev
Printer: Toppan Leefung Printing Ltd (China)

10 9 8 7 6 5 4 3 2 1

Keep up with New Holland Publishers on Facebook
www.facebook.com/NewHollandPublishers

Acknowledgements
I would like to thank my mother Jill and grandmother Adrianne for providing me with the inspiration
to write this book and for a love of fabric; my husband Mark for his support and encouragement and
looking after the children while I wrote it all down; my Dad Jimmy for giving me resilience, persistence
and strength; my daughters Ella and Tessa for their love; Michelle Leonard for strongly encouraging and
supporting me to get on with it!; Lliane Clarke for her many ideas and support; Fiona Schultz at New
Holland Publishers for agreeing to publish my work and the staff, Jodi De Vantier, Simona Hill and Tracy
Loughlin; Miranda Herron, Emma Virgona, Jan Redmond, Madeleine van Rijckervorsel and Maree
Knight and Lisa Nicol at the Back Room; Brooke Muckersie for my website, www.simplythis.com.au; Helen
Ashley for her mentoring; and Sue Stubbs for her intuitive photography.

I would like to thank the following suppliers: Linen Line Australia for supplying fabric to use in this book;
Reverse Garbage for recycled materials; The Vintage Shop for lampshades; The Salvation Army for fabric
and lampshades; Mitchel St Auction House for lamp bases; Spotlight for haberdashery supplies; Ikea for
basic homewares including curtains and pillowcases.

Contents

Introduction

Choosing and creating a style for your home decor and keeping within budget is a challenge for all of us. Yet, with even the smallest budget it's possible to create highly desirable soft furnishings that breathe life and colour into our homes and create comfort with their design, shape and texture.

I grew up on a farm and in a family in which most of my clothes were made by my mother. Out of necessity, she never wasted anything. Everything that could be recycled was taken apart and the good parts reused. Our lifestyle and circumstances challenged my mother to provide for the family in a creative way; it's a skill that I have inherited. I get my thriftiness from my mother. It was she who taught me the value of upcycling and I have a large stash of fabrics, trims, braids and buttons always ready to make and decorate projects as need and the desire dictate.

My grandmother also lived on a farm. She covered everyday items such as books and coathangers with material or card because she liked things to look pretty. She would reuse large canvas bags that were once full of sugar or flour and make them into small decorative bags, which she embellished with woollen embroidery, then used to store shoes or other items. My grandmother's skills, like women of her generation, were the product of the hardship caused by the Great Depression.

Women learned to 'make do and mend', using whatever material they could get their hands on to beautify their homes.

My mother taught me to embroider and do cross stitch, and I began to decorate my own fabrics, using these skills. I soon learned how to form simple decorative stitches and used them to beautify everyday items. Later, I learned to transform cloth with fabric paints, stencils, prints and dyes. Part of my love for colouring fabrics comes from the element of surprise of the dyeing techniques that I use. There is a random quality to dyeing fabric at home. Unwrapping the material once it is removed from the dye bath can bring some surprising results. This is known as mark-making in the textile industry. I am not alone in getting great satisfaction from doing this by hand — it is something really special. Every piece of fabric that we dye or print is unique and can rarely be produced again.

The advantage of using modern fabric paints and dyes is that it can be done at the kitchen table. It is quick to set up and you will already have many mark-making tools in your kitchen drawer. Don't be frightened by the paints and dyes — you can purchase these from your local craft store or online. They are inexpensive and offer a fast method by which to transform plain fabrics. They are also safe to use if you follow the manufacturer's instructions. I suggest that when you print or dye fabrics, you make an extra length for another project at the same time. Don't throw any fabric away. Even the smallest remnants have a use.

CHOOSING A PROJECT

The aim of this book is to show you how to decorate fabrics with prints, or dyes, or embellish them to make them into products for the home. Each

project that I have included is a celebration of fabric texture, colour and design. Some of the projects are easily achieveable over one day, others may take a weekend.

The projects are arranged according to their use within the different rooms of the home, and there's an extra chapter of personal and fun items that I love. As a mum, I spend a lot of time in the kitchen preparing meals for the family, catching up with my girlfriends and entertaining. For this room I have included stylish bowls, a pot holder, trivets, a French coffee press cosy, even a plastic bag holder. For the dining room I have created a sophisticated table runner and napkins. There's even a cutlery roll to take with you on a picnic.

I love cushions; they can be used to add a seasonal change to any room. For example, in autumn and winter I add cushions with warm and earthy tones to my living spaces, swapping them from the fresh neutral palette with which I furnish the home in spring and summer. Ringing the changes in this way is relatively inexpensive and fun to do, expecially if you make the furnishings yourself.

My bedroom is a calm and peaceful sanctuary. For this room I have included ideas to decorate pillows, curtains, cushions and a bedside lampshade.

Some of the projects remind me of my youth — covered coathangers that my mother made and journal covers that my grandmother would have loved. There's a fun shower cap too, as well as fabric baskets in which you can store all manner of paraphernalia, a nod to the memory of my grandmother.

HOW TO USE THIS BOOK

If you love the soft furnishing ideas in this book but don't want to print or dye the fabric, go ahead! The project patterns all standalone. In fact, I've included one or two projects that don't require any fabric printing or dyeing at all. However, if the opportunity to add colour or ring the changes to existing textiles is just too great, I have included plenty of fun methods to create decorative fabric, including printing with wooden blocks, toilet rolls, a sponge or egg ring, the edge of a ruler or with bubble wrap. All produce different results. Stencilling is a skill that is easy to master. I show you how to create stencils using a craft knife, self-healing cutting mat and thick plastic. I also show you how to use a paper doily as a stencil — it creates a lovely lacy effect on fabric — or if you prefer geometric designs, how to use masking tape to mask off areas of fabric and brush colour into the remaining areas.

First choose a project that you'd like to make, then decide which printing, dyeing or embellishment technique suits that project. Feel free to experiment with the different techniques, or combine them. Cushion covers, for example, may be printed, dyed or embellished — or a combination of all three!

Basic sewing skills are all you'll require for each project. I've deliberately kept them simple. I do suggest you to use a sewing machine in the sewing projects however, as it speeds up the process.

Don't feel like sewing? For some of the projects no sewing is needed. The embellished lampshade, for example, requires frayed fabrics and a hot glue gun.

I love textiles. They make me happy and I hope my enthusiasm rubs off on you. I wish you as much pleasure in making and creating these projects as I had in designing these fabrics and projects for you and your home.

Tools and Materials

Craft projects all require a multitude of equipment. Very few specialist items are required for the projects in this book, and many of the required tools will already be in your kitchen drawers.

To draw a stencil design you'll need an HB pencil, tracing paper, scissors, thick sheets of plastic to cut the stencil from, a self-healing cutting mat on which to cut the plastic and a craft knife.

I find the best place to paint fabric is at the kitchen table, although any large flat surface where there's a good source of light will do. If I am dyeing fabric, I prefer to work outside because any spills will stain the floor. Protect the work surface with newspaper so that you don't damage it. I put a cheap plastic throwaway tablecloth on top of the newspaper and use masking tape to hold it in place. If you are painting or dyeing fabric you'll need to be close to a sink.

For fabric painting you will need some inexpensive paint brushes – one or two small, medium and large sizes for applying and mixing paints.

Water-based fabric paint is available in 75 ml (2½ fl oz) tubes or 300 ml (½ pint) pots from craft shops, art suppliers or online and in a huge assortment of colours. I use Permaset Fabric Printing Colour, which is made permanent by ironing the dried paint with a hot iron. After ironing the print is wash-, dry clean- and rub-resistant. Always read the manufacturer's instructions for use since brands and products vary. You will also need a container in which to mix paint, plastic or glass pots with lids in which to store mixed paint, and your chosen printing tool. For printing, you will need a paint tray (I use a baking tray) that is big enough to accommodate the print tool.

For shibori dyeing you will need 10 blocks of wood, each 10 cm (4 in) long and 1 cm (³/8 in) thick. You'll also need a bucket in which to mix the dye. If you choose one that has a lid, you'll be able to store any unused dye for another project. You'll also need a large bag of plastic cable ties to secure the wood blocks to the fabric and a packet of fabric dye. For shibori, I use the traditional dark blue colour, denim blue. I use Rit dye, but any other brand will work well. For 3 m (3 yd) of fabric a 30 g (1 oz) sachet is sufficient. You'll also need a stick to mix the dye bath. To protect your clothes and skin wear a plastic apron and plastic gloves.

The cloth you choose to work with and from which you will make your project is important. Some dyes and paints will not take to fabrics that contain synthetic or manmade elements, or they may produce a much paler version of the colour you were hoping for. I love using 100 per cent linen and/or silk. These fabrics have a luxurious quality, and has a more open woven texture, which lends itself to producing some interesting effects with print and dye. Because they are a natural product the colour density will be strong.

If you are going to launder the finished item, you will need to wash and dry the fabric before you colour it. Press the fabric using an iron on an ironing board so that it is crease-free before you begin. For fixing (setting) fabric paints, I also recommend that you have an old cloth that you put over the paint to protect the surface of the iron. You don't need to wash the fabric for other projects such as lampshades.

A sewing machine is an essential tool. Though you could hand sew each item, if you like, a sewing machine will certainly speed up the process. Choose a sewing thread that is natural if you are working with natural fabrics – cotton is fine and will accept fabric dye or paint. Your sewing kit will ideally include a fabric marker, a selection of sewing needles, fabric scissors, a ruler, a tape measure, a quick unpick and pins.

Finally, to make and decorate the projects an assortment of ribbons, braids, buttons, bias binding, zippers and velcro are used. Some projects require wadding (batting), household brown string, elastic bands, spray glue, a hot glue gun and hot glue sticks.

Elements of Design

Unless you're making a project in which the design is to be printed all over – using bubble wrap, for instance – there are a few things to consider before you get busy with the paint.

Do you want an all-over design, in which the motifs are evenly spaced across and along the fabric? If this is what you're after, then using a fabric marker to lightly mark the position of each motif on the fabric may produce a more even result than placing a motif by eye, especially if you're not quite sure if you'll get the spacing accurate. Harmonious designs with evenly-spaced motifs have a rhythm that the eye moves over with ease. These motifs can be any shape, but are usually in proportion with an amount of space around that the eye can rest upon. These designs may look simple, but the larger the piece of fabric, the more work will be required to make sure you have a balanced design. If you're incorporating more than one motif into the design, look at how the shapes work together as well as how they work within the space. Check too that the space around them makes an interesting shape.

Choose a motif that is an apropriate scale for the item that you are making. A finished small-scale item will look odd if it has an over-sized motif on it that can't be seen clearly. Similarly, a very large item with a very small motif will have no momentum and the motif may become lost within the fabric.

Geometric designs may be a good choice for a first project since the shapes you use have a strong design presence. If you want a bold effect, often a large-scale motif is required. Alternatively, if you are want a subtle, muted effect then the motif will be smaller in scale and possibly lighter in tone.

I suggest that you practise on paper before you start printing on cloth so that you can see how the design elements work together with each other and with your chosen colour. Take your time, and try the design on a scrap of fabric. The fabric texture may affect how much paint you need to use, or how firmly you press on the printing tool.

COLOUR

Another consideration is the colour that you will use for the design. You may be designing a project to co-ordinate with existing furnishings, so trialling different colour or tone combinations and leaving them to dry so that you're sure they will dry to the shade that you want is important. Some fabric paints dry to a darker tone than their wet colour, while others are lighter once they are dry. The base colour of the fabric also affects the finished colour.

Printing tone on tone, meaning choosing a paint colour that is very similar to the fabric colour you are printing on, will give you a very subtle effect. If you are making a range of projects for a room, try to co-ordinate the colours or motifs so that the items look good when placed together.

Whatever colour I use I always start with less paint on the brush and add layers by degrees to see what the effect is. Some motifs may require gradation of paint to create depth and variation to the design.

Upcycling and Embellishment

'Upcycling' is a modern term coined to describe a process of transforming old and unloved objects into new ones. The 'new' items ideally will have a perceived greater worth or beauty than the original. A patchwork quilt, for instance, made from aged and much-loved fabrics can become a desirable object if the elements of its design are carefully thought through and executed. Though the term upcycling is relatively new, the concept is not and the trend is growing. Not only does upcycling provide an opportunity to create 'new' items for little financial outlay, the added benefit is that it has little or no environmental impact. If we remake the old, then we don't need to buy new. Added to this is the pleasure to be had in making something, whether the appeal is creative, financial or environmental.

The quickest and easiest way to upcycle an item is to add embellishments to it. These can be as simple as adding beading or braid to a collar or lampshade, dyeing items of home furnishings where the fabric is still good but the colour may no longer be to our taste, stitching an embroidery design on plain curtains, or adding a whole host of other design details such as braids, torn and frayed fabric strips, ribbons and buttons — whatever is appropriate for the item and the look that you want to create.

Once you have decided what you are going to embellish and how, set some time aside to plan and shop for the items you need. The trick with upcycling is to make the finished object look as if it always had the embellishment that you have given it, so the finish of the item is very important. Make sure you remove loose threads, minimise excess glue and tie your embroidery threads off neatly so they don't come undone.

Brand new items such as pillowcases or cushions can also be upcycled to coordinate with the rest of your bedding. These items make great personalised gift or keepsakes.

I spend hours in secondhand and recycling shops looking for things that I can give a new life to or alter to make something totally different. You can pick up great fabrics from upholstery shops — look for discontinued ranges or even old sample books, which often get thrown away. Another place to pick up fabric is at an local alterations shop. I love collecting different coloured denims, usually the bottoms of jeans that have been shortened. There are many hues of blue, which can be patched together to create a new fabric.

I also collect vintage tea towels and put them in picture frames, arranging them as a group. You could do the same with hand-crocheted or embroidered work. The craftmanship of old items is often beautifully executed — these are valued special items and have often been well looked after. Framing a collection of similar items can create great textile art for your living spaces for little financial outlay. Other people's trash can be your treasure — you just need to think creatively how you might use it to positive effect.

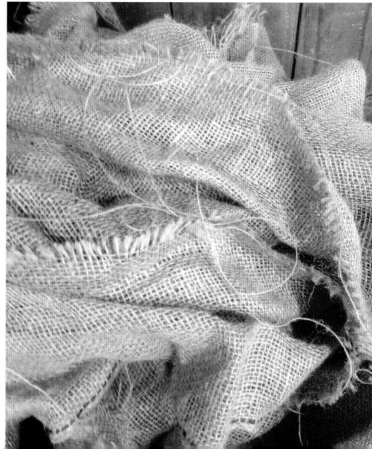

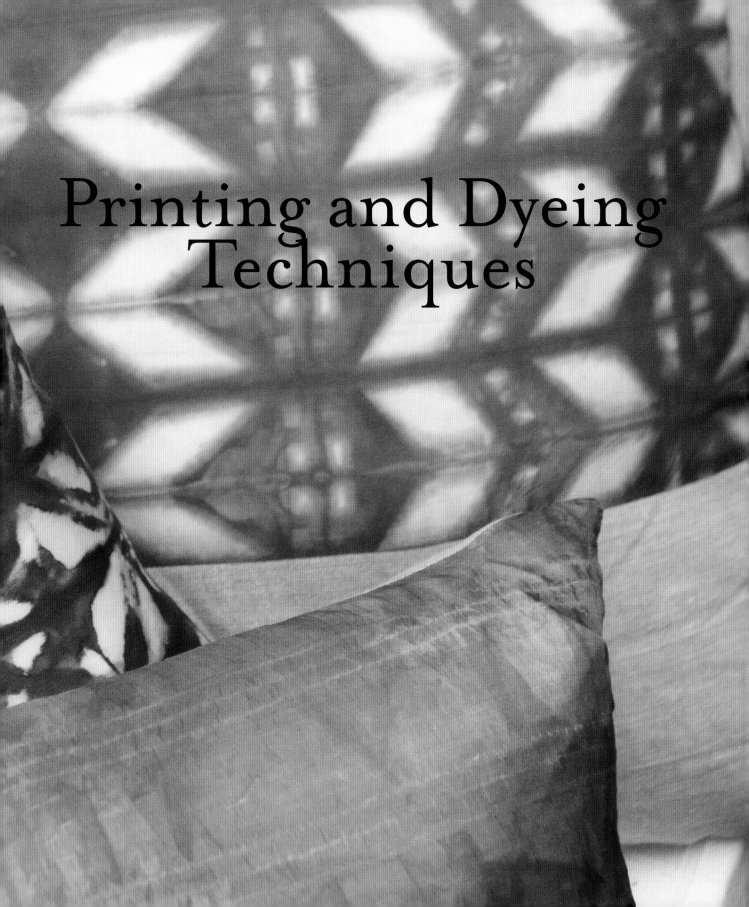

Printing and Dyeing Techniques

Printing with Wooden Blocks

You will need

Protective cover for the work surface
Iron and ironing board
Linen or other natural fabric
Fabric paints, two colours, 1 x 300 ml
(½ pint) pot each will be plenty to
start with
Baking tray (sheet)
Paint brush
Wood blocks

The blocks that I have used are shibori-dyeing wooden blocks. They are about 10 cm (4 in) long and 1 cm (³/₈ in) wide. This method lends itself to repetition and regular designs.

1 Cover the work surface to protect it. Iron the fabric to remove any creases and arrange on the work surface.

2 Tip some fabric paint onto the baking tray, add a little water and mix with a paint brush to a runny consistency. I have used two different colours on this design.

3 Using the paintbrush apply paint evenly to one face of the wood block. Press down onto the fabric. Repeat, changing colour every third or fourth print for added visual interest.

4 As you work down the fabric, change the proportion of colours to give variation to the design. Continue until you reach the end of the fabric. Leave to dry completely, then press to set the paint following the manufacturer's instructions.

Projects decorated with this technique
Tea towels, bolster cushion, cushion cover.

Printing with Toilet Rolls

You will need

Protective cover for the work surface
Masking tape
Iron and ironing board
Linen or cotton fabric
Elastic band
Toilet rolls
Fabric paint, 1 x 300 ml (½ pint) pot
    will be plenty to start with
Flat plate, for mixing paint
Paint brush, to mix the paint
Scrap paper

You might find it surprising that a toilet roll makes a perfect printing tool! The interesting thing about this printing tool is that the mark it creates is organic and textured and each stamp on the fabric will be slightly different. The effect will vary on different weights and textures of paper, just as it will with different types and weights of fabric.

1 Secure the protective cover to the work surface with masking tape. Iron the fabric and ensure it is crease free or the creases will affect the finished look of the printing. Wrap an elastic band around the end of the toilet roll to stop the layers from unravelling.

2 Pour some fabric paint onto a flat plate and dilute it with water so that it is a little runny like thin cream and soaks into the toilet roll. If you are mixing paints to create a new shade, mix enough for the entire project. Test the colour density on paper or a scrap of fabric to make sure you are happy with it. Leave it to dry to see if the colour changes, expecially if you are matching this colour to other accessories.

3 Consider how your design will appear on the fabric — random printings or groups of motifs that flow across the fabric, for example. Start printing, reapplying paint every couple of prints to keep the motif consistent throughout the design.

4 Leave the paint to dry completely, then press with an iron to set it according to the paint manufacturer's instructions.

Projects decorated with this technique
Tea towels, cushion cover.

Printing with a Sponge and Egg Ring

You will need

Protective cover for the work surface
Masking tape
Iron and ironing board
Fabric
Pencil
Cup
Sponge
Scissors
Fabric paint, 1 x 300 ml (½ pint) pot
    will be plenty to start with
Flat plate, for mixing paint
Paint brush, for mixing paint
Scrap paper and fabric
Egg ring

Egg rings create marks that look like organic circles. I find the slightly irregular circle pleasing. In contrast, a circle of sponge used as a printing tool leaves a softly textured shape on the surface of the fabric that can be used to create interesting designs. Sponges can be cut to any shape and since they are available in different densities, each will produce a different effect.

1 Secure the protective cover to the work surface with masking tape. Iron the fabric and ensure it is crease free or the creases will affect the finished look of the printing.

2 Using a pencil and a cup as a guide draw circles on the sponge and cut them out.

3 Pour some fabric paint onto a flat plate and dilute it with water so that it is a little runny like thin cream and will show the texture of the sponge when printed. If you are mixing paints to create a new shade, mix enough for the entire project. Test the colour density on paper or a scrap of fabric to make sure you are happy with it and get a feel for how hard to press the sponge.

4 Test print the egg ring and sponge on paper and scrap fabric to make sure you are happy with the effect. Start with the sponge – press gently into the paint and then on to the fabric. Repeat, reapplying the paint every couple of prints to keep the intensity of colour consistent throughout the design.

5 Next, using the egg ring, print over the sponge-printed motifs to create contrast and another dimension to the design. Leave the paint to dry, then press with an iron to set the fabric paint according to the manufacturer's instructions.

Projects decorated with this technique
Tea towels, shower cap, lampshade.

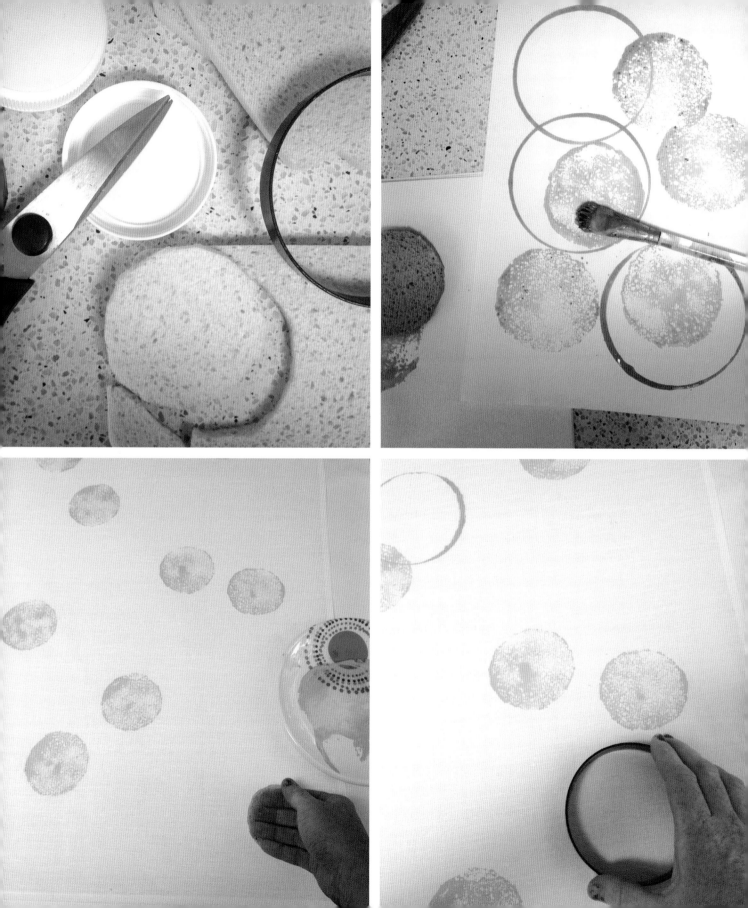

Printing with Masking Tape

This technique is great for creating striped fabric. Masking tape literally masks off areas that will not be painted. You can play with the thickness of the stripe and its regularity. Paint is applied by brushing it onto the fabric with a dry brush, allowing scope to vary the colours within the stripe as well as the paint density. Use a textured fabric for an interesting effect.

1 Cover the work surface with protective paper or plastic. Press the fabric to remove any creases and arrange flat on the work surface.

2 Decide how thick the painted stripes will be and whether the pattern will be regular and even or random stripes. Mark the distance between each stripe on the fabric using a tape measure and pencil.

3 Stick the masking tape in place on each of your marked lines, keeping the tape as straight as possible. Run your hand over the tape to make sure that it is stuck securely to the fabric to stop any paint from bleeding underneath.

4 Tip some paint onto a plate, then load the paintbrush. Brush off any excess paint on paper so that the brush is almost dry – you'll get an even application of paint this way.

5 Apply the paint to the fabric, brushing it between the masking tape guides. Build up layers of colour density by applying more paint. It is a good idea to practise first on a scrap of fabric before you do the whole piece.

6 Leave to dry completely, then peel off the masking tape. Press to set the paint according to the manufacturer's instructions.

Projects decorated with this technique
Doorstop, cutlery roll, apron, door snake, fabric baskets.

You will need

Protective cover for the work surface
Fabric
Iron and ironing board
Tape measure
Pencil
Masking tape
Fabric paint, 1 x 300 ml (½ pint) pot
will be plenty to start with
Plate, for mixing paint
Paint brush with thick bristles
Scrap paper

Printing with Paper Doilies

Paper doilies can be used as a stencil to create a soft feminine pattern on fabric. Overlay doilies and play with the intensity of paint to give variation and interest to your design.

1 Secure the protective cover to the work surface with masking tape. Iron the fabric and ensure it is crease free or the creases will affect the finished look of the printing.

2 Cut the centre from each of the paper doilies, varying the size of the cut-away centre. Lightly spray the back of each with glue and stick in place on the fabric. The glue will help keep the doilies in place while you print.

3 Pour fabric paint into the plate. Dip the sponge into the paint and remove the excess by dabbing the sponge on scrap paper. This will help to distribute the paint evenly on the sponge before printing.

4 Dab the sponge lightly and evenly over the doilies to create the design. Lightly dab around the outer edge of some doilies to create a shadow effect, if you like.

5 Remove the paper doilies and leave the paint to dry. Press with an iron to set the colour into the fabric, according to the paint manufacturer's instructions. This is not an exacting technique and you can overlay the print to cover any imperfections.

Projects decorated with this technique
Journal cover, shower cap.

You will need

Protective cover for the work surface
Masking tape
Iron and ironing board
Cotton or linen fabric
Paper scissors
3 paper doilies, approximately 15 cm (6 in) diameter
Spray glue
Fabric paints, 1 x 300 ml (½ pint) pot will be plenty to start with
Plastic plate, for mixing paint
Sponge
Scrap paper

Printing with the Edge of a Ruler

You will need

Paper to protect the work surface
Masking tape
Linen fabric
Iron and ironing board
Fabric paint, 1 x 300 ml (½ pint) pot
    will be plenty to start with
Baking tray (sheet), at least 30 cm
    (12 in) long
30 cm (12 in) ruler
Scissors
Apron

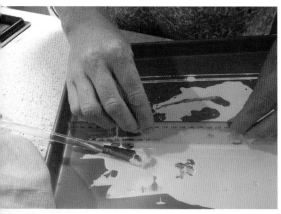

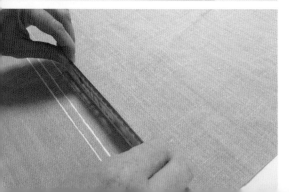

Everyone has a ruler stashed in a drawer. For this technique a plastic ruler is best just because it'll be easier to clean.

1 Arrange the paper so that it completely covers the work surface and secure it in place with masking tape so that it won't move around.

2 Iron the fabric to remove any creases and arrange on the protected work surface.

3 Tip some fabric paint into the tray and add a little water to make a runny consistency. Make sure the paint spreads out to the edges so that you can fit the length of the ruler in the tray.

4 Put one long edge of the ruler into the paint. Ensure the entire edge has paint on it. Tap the ruler a couple of times over the tray to remove any excess.

5 Press the ruler onto the fabric. Move the ruler up the fabric and make another print, offsetting it slightly from the first print. I used the grain of the fabric as a guide to keep my lines relatively straight.

Projects decorated with this technique
Table runner, napkins.

Printing with Stencils

You will need

Pencil
Paper
Plastic sheet, 100 microns thick
Craft knife and self-healing cutting mat
Iron and ironing board
Linen or cotton fabric
Scissors
Fabric paint, 1 x 300 ml (½ pint) pot
    will be plenty to start with
Scrap fabric
Plate, for mixing paint
Thick paint brush or sponge
Old cloth

A stencil is a plastic sheet with a shape cut from its centre. Stencils can be reused repeatedly to rapidly produce identical motifs that appear as silhouettes on the printed surface. They are created with a brush, but they can also be applied with a sponge or dry brush to create a textured effect.

1 Draw your chosen motif on paper. You could trace around a shape or draw a freehand image. Place the plastic sheet over the image.

2 Use a craft knife to cut out the motif, using a cutting mat to protect the work surface. Discard the inner part of the motif. The area around the motif becomes the stencil.

3 Iron the fabric to remove any creases. Think about the placement of the motif on the fabric and the space needed between each image to create a balanced design. Grouping the images can create a more interesting design, which allows the eye to flow across the fabric.

4 Tip some fabric paint onto a plate; it should be the consistency of thick custard. Test your design first on scrap paper or fabric. Pick up some paint with a thick paint brush and remove the excess on scrap paper. Painting will create an even print with a clearly defined outline. Dabbing will create a textured effect.

5 Place the template in the desired position, hold securely in place and apply the paint. Move your image to the next position and repeat the process until you have covered the fabric.

6 Leave the paint to dry. Put the fabric paint side up on the ironing board, cover with an old cloth over to protect the iron and press to set the fabric according to the paint manufacturer's instructions.

Projects decorated with this technique
Christmas decorations Christmas stocking.

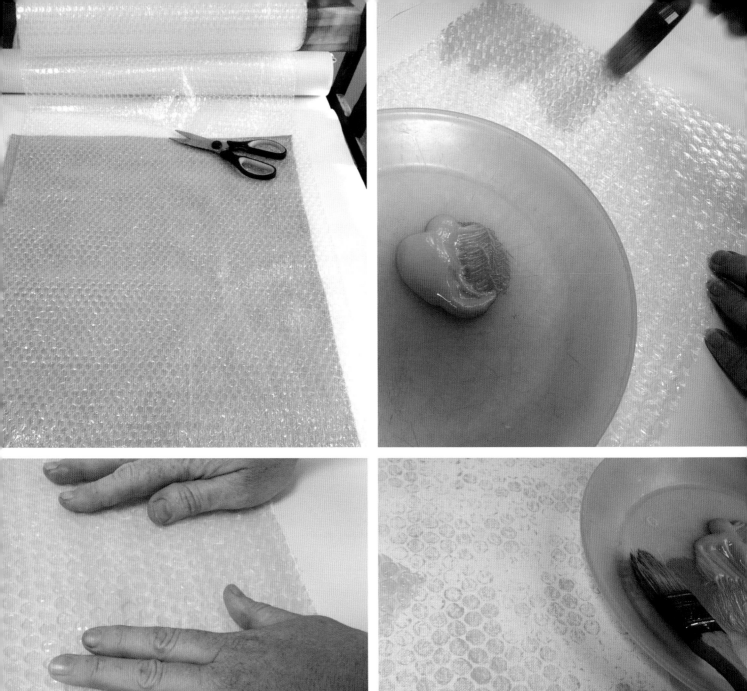
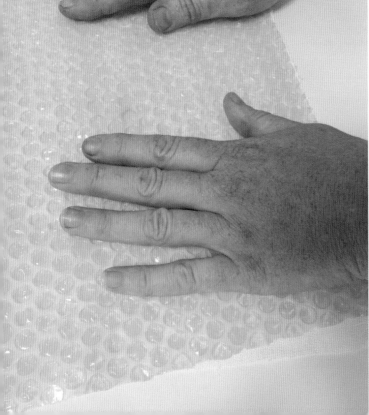

Printing with Bubble Wrap

This method is great on a textured piece of fabric and is useful to coordinate with other printed designs. You will not get a precise print because of the nature of the printing surface — it's very difficult to get an even distribution of paint from the plastic to the fabric.

1 Protect the work surface with a layer of plastic and then paper to absorb any paint that soaks through the fabric when printing. The surface should be smooth and big enough to accommodate a large piece of fabric.

2 Iron the fabric to remove any creases, then arrange on the protected work surface. Cut the bubble wrap into a shapes, if you like, or work with a large length of bubble wrap if you want to cover a large area of fabric.

3 Tip fabric paint onto a flat plate and use the paint brush to apply to the bubble wrap. Make a test print to make sure that you are happy with the density and distribution of colour.

4 When you are happy with the print effect, print the bubble wrap on to the fabric to gently transfer the paint to the fabric. It will be slippery so try not to move the plastic around when printing or it will blur the print.

5 Leave the fabric to dry, then press with an iron to set the paint, following the paint manufacturer's instructions.

Projects decorated with this technique
Cutlery roll, cushion, pot holder, fabric basket.

You will need

Paper and plastic to protect the work surface
Iron and ironing board
Fabric
Scissors
Bubble wrap
Fabric paint, 1 x 300 ml (½ pint) pot will be plenty to start with
Flat plate, for mixing paint

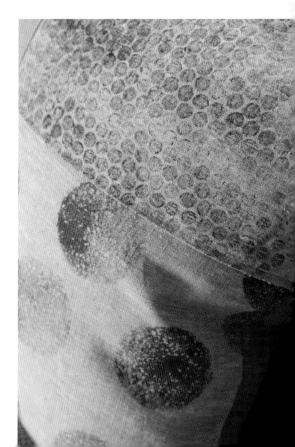

Japanese Shibori Resist Dyeing

Shibori is a traditional Japanese technique of creating patterns on fabric by clamping, twisting, stitching, folding and wrapping fabric, then placing it into a vat of dye. The areas of cloth that are tied become impenetrable to the fabric dye. There are many methods of binding the cloth and each creates a different pattern on the finished dyed cloth. Traditionally this dye would have been made from the indigo plant. Today, we can use commercial dyes to create a very similar effect. I love unravelling the dyed fabric. It's a bit like unwrapping a present — you're never quite sure what to expect. Every piece of shibori is unique and that makes it special. I find silk produces the best results because it can be clamped and compressed very tightly, which creates a well-defined and even print.

1 Cut a piece of fabric to the length required for the project. Fold the fabric concertina-style, starting at one end and making the folds 5–6 cm (2–2½ in) wide. Press each fold with an iron as you go.

2 Clamp the fabric between two wooden blocks and secure with plastic ties. Make sure you clamp the fabric as tightly as possible to stop the dye penetrating the fabric.

3 Place the next wood blocks at an angle across the folded layers of fabric to create a different pattern. Secure with ties, string or elastic bands at each end of the wooden blocks. Continue to work across the folded fabric.

4 Alternatively, you could wrap a piece of string around the fabric, instead of using wood blocks, which will leave a different mark. Tie the string as tightly as you can to resist the dye.

You will need

Silk, silk satin, cotton or rayon fabric
Fabric scissors
Iron and ironing board
Wooden blocks approximately
10 cm (4 in) long
Plastic cable ties or string or elastic
bands to tie the
wood blocks to the fabric
Fabric dye
Bucket, for the dye
Stick, for mixing dye
Clothes airer
Dye fixative

Below: Mixing the dye the traditional way.

5 Mix the dye in the bucket according to the manufacturer's instructions.

6 Place the clamped fabric bundles into the dye bucket. The longer you leave the fabric in the dye the more intense the resulting colour will be. Add three or four scraps of fabric to the bucket, then remove each at different time intervals so you can get a sense of the strength of colour.

7 After you pull the fabric out, undo the wood blocks and string and hang on the line or over a clothes rack until it dries.

8 You may need to use a fixative so follow the manufacturer's instructions to set the dye.

Projects decorated with this technique
Wheat bag, scarf, tea towel, cushion covers.

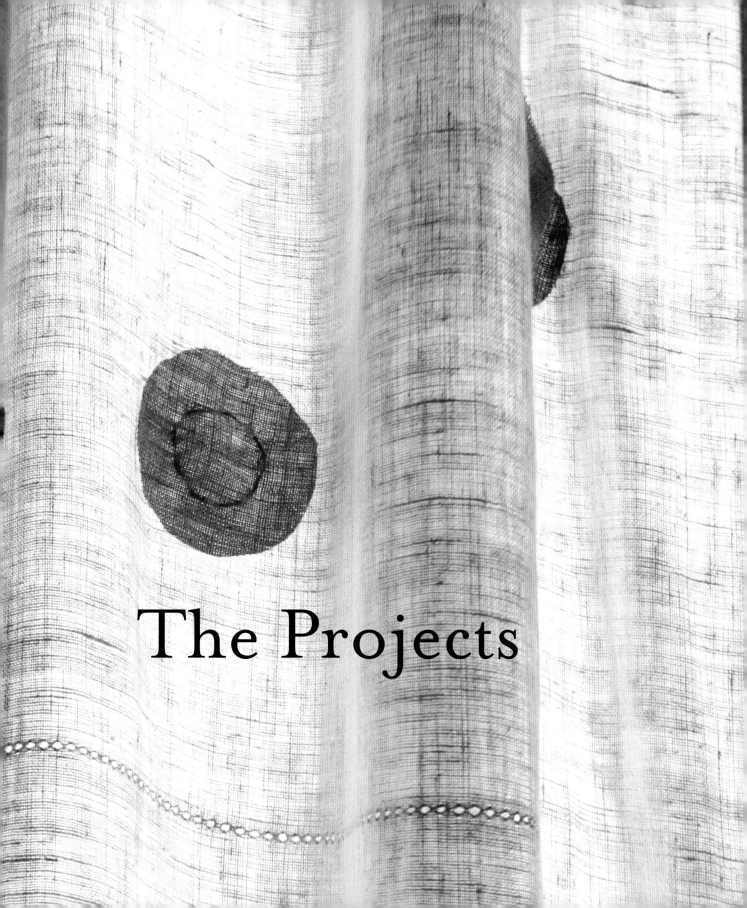

The Projects

Kitchen

French Coffee Press Cosy

Tape measure
Pencil and paper
Wadding (batting) (optional)
Fabric scissors
Scraps of co-ordinating fabric
Iron and ironing board
Backing fabric
Sewing machine
Thread
String or thin ribbon
Pins

I love coffee and like to drink it in leisurely fashion. In order to help keep the coffee warm, I made an upcycled cosy using scraps of fabric.

1 To work out the dimensions of the finished cosy, first measure the height of the coffee press from beneath the pouring lip to the base and note your measurement. Measure around the circumference of the coffee press, not including the handle area, and note the measure.

2 Cut a piece of wadding to the dimensions of the measurement if you are using lightweight fabrics. Cut a piece of backing fabric, adding 3 cm (1¼ in) to the length and height of your measurement for seam allowances. Press in a small hem all around.

3 Cut the scrap fabrics into strips, each 3 cm (1¼ in) longer than the height measurement of the coffee press, to allow for seam allowances. My strips were 5 cm (2 in) wide. Some of my strips have frayed edges, which I used as a design feature.

4 Arrange the strips right side up and overlapping slightly. There should be enough strips to fit around the circumference of the coffee press, plus a 3 cm (1¼ in) seam allowance. The overlapping will help provide insulation.

5 Press the strips, pin and then stitch them together using straight or zigzag stitch on the sewing maching using a matching thread. Press again. Turn in to the wrong side a 1.5 cm ($^{5}/_{8}$ in) seam allowance at the top and bottom of the panel.

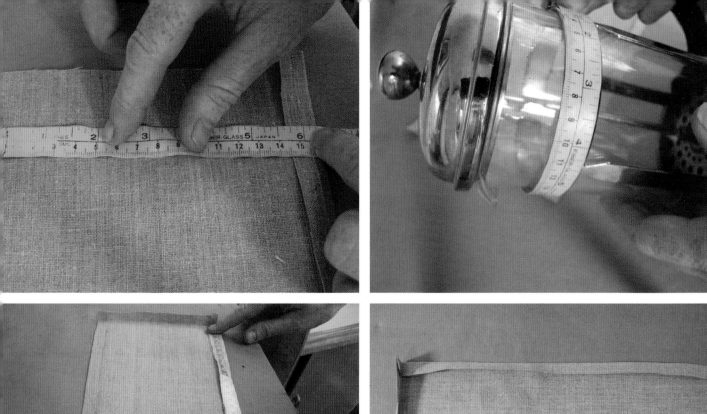

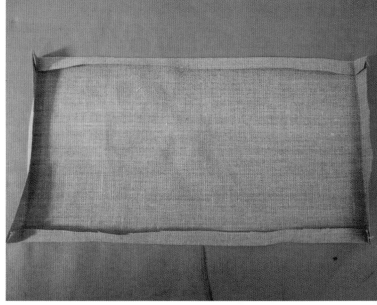

6 Cut two lengths of string or ribbon the circumference of the coffee press plus enough extra to tie a bow comfortably. Arrange the string or ribbon just inside the pressed seam allowance and pin or stitch in place.

7 Centre the wadding on the wrong side of the backing fabric, if using, and pin in place from the right side.

8 Place the pieced panel and backing fabric right sides together (with the wadding, if using on the outside of the backing fabric). Stitch the layers together, allowing a 1.5 cm ($^5/_8$ in) seam allowance and leaving a small opening in one long edge to turn through. Backstitch into the corners to reinforce the stitching.

9 Turn through, press and slipstitch the opening closed. Press. Tie around the cosy.

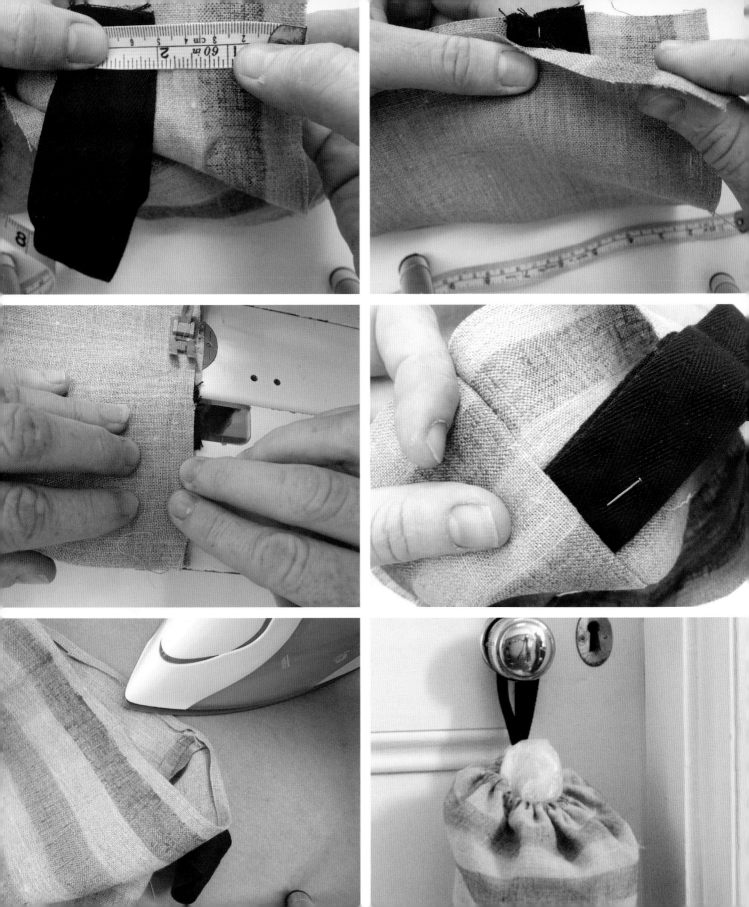

Plastic Bag Holder

Useful to hold all those surplus carrier bags in one place, this plastic bag holder can be hung in the kitchen or laundry room for easy access. Why not co-ordinate the colour scheme with those of your tea towels or pot holder? For this project I have used the masking tape-printing method.

1 Fold the ribbon or tape in half to form a hanging loop and stitch to the side seam, 5 cm (2 in) from the top raw edge (the top is a short end).

2 Fold the printed fabric in half along the short edge, with right sides together and raw edges aligned. Sew the 70 cm (27½ in) edges together using a 1.5 cm (⅝ in) seam allowance. Backstitch over the hanging loop to strengthen it.

3 Turn in a 0.5 cm (¼ in) hem at the top and bottom raw edges and press in place. Turn in another hem at 1.5 cm (⅝ in) and press. Unpick the seam to create an opening into the channel. Stitch in place close to the turned edge to create a small channel through which to thread the elastic.

4 Use a safety pin to pin through the elastic and thread it through the channel. Stitch both ends of the elastic together and then close the small opening with a slipstitch using a needle and thread.

You will need

Masking tape-printed fabric,
70 x 50 cm (27½ x 20 in)
Sewing machine
Thread
Ribbon or tape, 20 cm (8 in)
Elastic, 2, lengths each 20 x 1 cm
(8 x ⅜ in) wide
Safety pin
Sewing needle

Apron

I have used the masking tape-printing technique for this project, which features a masking tape-printed pocket on a plain apron. The amount of ink is graded so that each stripe had a variation in density. I have co-ordinated the colours of my ties with the print colour used on the pocket.

1 Cut one pocket for the apron from printed fabric 23 x 23 cm (9 x 9 in).

2 From the ribbon, cut two lengths each 1 m (39 in) for the ties and one length 56 cm (22 in) for the neck strap.

3 Using the diagram and the measurements provided in the templates (p 172), draft a pattern on paper, add 1.5 cm (⁵/₈ in) all around for seam allowances and then cut out your apron.

4 Turn in and press 0.75 cm (¼ in) all around the apron, then turn in and press 0.75 cm (¼ in) again and topstitch all around the apron using matching thread. Trim any hanging threads and press.

5 Turn in and press a 0.75cm (¼ in) seam allowance all around the pocket, then turn in and press 0.75 cm (¼ in) again. Topstitch the top edge of the pocket to finish off the opening.

6 Pin and stitch the pocket to the apron, following the pattern as a guide. Topstitch the sides and bottom of the pocket, backstitching at the beginning and end to reinforce the stitching.

7 Turn in and press a small hem on the ribbon ends. Stitch to the neck and waist of the apron. Backstitch to strengthen the stitching.

8 I have added extra ribbon to create a loop design detail at the front of the apron. Backstitch to strengthen. Press.

You will need

Masking-tape printed linen , 23 x 23cm (9 x 9 in)

Linen, 1.5 x 1.2 m (60 x 48 in)

Fabric scissors

Ribbon, 2.6 m (2¾ yd) x 4 cm (1½ in) wide

Fabric

Paper, to make a pattern

Pencil

Tape measure

Iron and ironing board

Sewing machine

Matching thread

Fabric Trivet

You will need

Fabric scissors
Fabric, in an assortment of lengths
Hot glue gun
Glue

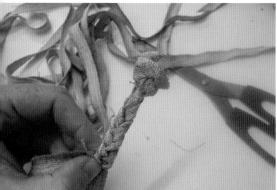

Lengths of fabric are plaited (braided) together. The plait is then formed into a circle and held in place with glue.

1 Cut the fabric into strips approximately 2 cm (¾ in) thick. If you want the finished mat to be thicker, cut the fabric strips wider.

2 Tie three strips of fabric together at one end of the lengths with a knot that is tight and flat.

3 Plait (braid) the strips. You will find that when you get to the end of the fabric it will be uneven. Extend any strip by plaiting new lengths with the old one. Do this for each strip. The more you plait the bigger the mat. For my mat I plaited 2 m (78 in).

4 When you have finished plaiting, join the three strips together with hot glue, following the manufacturer's instructions, and trim any excess fabric.

5 Use the knotted end to start turning and gluing the plait into a circle. Work in small sections so that the glue doesn't dry before the fabric is secured. Tuck the end under to finish and glue it flat.

Bowls

Assortment of fabric lengths
Scissors
Hot glue gun
Glue sticks
Sturdy glass or plastic bowl
Scissors

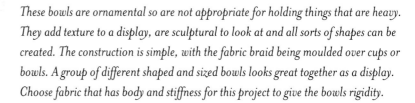

These bowls are ornamental so are not appropriate for holding things that are heavy. They add texture to a display, are sculptural to look at and all sorts of shapes can be created. The construction is simple, with the fabric braid being moulded over cups or bowls. A group of different shaped and sized bowls looks great together as a display. Choose fabric that has body and stiffness for this project to give the bowls rigidity.

1 Cut or tear the fabric into strips 2 cm (¾ in) wide. You may need approximately 2–3 m (2–3 yd) depending on the size of your finished bowl.

2 Tie the ends of three pieces of fabric together with a tight knot. Plait (braid) the fabric strips, keeping it as neat and even as possible.

3 When you get to the end of one strip add another to it with hot glue. Keep plaiting until you think you have enough to make a bowl. You can add more when you are constructing the bowl, if necessary.

4 Beginning with the knotted end, start to form the plait into a circle gluing it into a disk shape. Work on the thin side of the plait so the bowl is thinner and takes less plaiting to complete.

5 Turn the bowl upside down on the work surface. Place the glued disk onto the base of the bowl and wrap the plait around the bowl, sticking the layers together as you work and using the bowl shape as a mould.

6 When you reach the top, trim the end of the plait so that it is neat and glue in place. Remove it from the mould before it is completely dry, or you may damage the mould when trying to remove it.

Pot Holder

You will need

8 strips of bubble wrap-printed and
    masking tape-printed fabric with
    assorted prints at least 3 cm (1¼ in)
    wide x 24 cm (9½ in) long
Fabric scissors
1 piece of backing fabric 24 x 24 cm
    (9½ x 9½ in)
Pins
Wadding (batting)
Bias binding
Sewing machine
Matching thread

I have used fabric remnants left over from other projects to make the front of this pot holder and have included a mixture of masking tape and bubble wrap printed fabric. Keep all your scraps from other printing projects because they may end up being used for something really special. For a gift, you could co-ordinate your fabric and create a matching tea towel and pot holder.

1 Fringe some of the fabric lengths by teasing out 4 or 5 threads from one long edge.

2 Overlap the strips of fabric right side up and arrange them into a 24 cm (9½ in) square, spacing them evenly. When you are happy with the arrangement, pin and then stitch the strips together. If you are using fabrics that may fray, use zig-zag stitches to help stop the fraying. Clip all the loose threads and press.

3 Cut a piece of wadding 24 x 24 cm (9½ x 9½ in).

4 Place the backing fabric right side down. Top with the wadding, then the stitched fabric right side up. Pin all the layers together and sew at 5 mm (¼ in) from the edge to sandwich all the layers together.

5 For the hanging loop, cut a piece of bias binding 12 cm (5 in) long. Fold in half and align the raw edges with one corner of the pot holder. Stitch in place.

6 Bind the edges of the pot holder with bias binding, ensuring you catch in all three layers.

Dining Room

Napkins

You will need

Printed linen
Iron and ironing board
Tape measure
Sewing machine
Matching thread
Scissors

This is a relatively quick project to make and looks great if you co-ordinate the print with that of a table runner. I have used the sponge-printing method for this project.

1 Cut 6 pieces of printed linen 47 x 45.5 cm (18½ x 18 in) and press to remove any creases.

2 Turn in 0.75 cm (¼ in) all around the edge of each napkin and press with a hot iron. Turn in the same amount again and press.

3 Open out and trim across the corners diagonally, close to the pressed corner, to reduce bulk. Refold the napkins, then topstitch the hem using matching thread. Reverse stitch at the start and finish to reinforce the stitching.

Table Runner

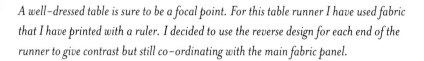

You will need

Tape measure
Ruler-printed fabric
Contrast fabric
Backing fabric
Thread
Sewing machine
Scissors
Iron and ironing board

A well-dressed table is sure to be a focal point. For this table runner I have used fabric that I have printed with a ruler. I decided to use the reverse design for each end of the runner to give contrast but still co-ordinating with the main fabric panel.

1 Measure the length of the table, then take 80 cm (31½ in) from this measurement to give the length of the centre panel. Cut one piece of print fabric to this length x 43 cm (17 in) wide.

2 Cut two end panels 43 x 43 cm (17 x 17 in) from contrast fabric.

3 Pin and then stitch the centre panel to an end panel, right sides together, using a 1.5 cm (⁵/8 in) seam allowance. Open the seam and press. Repeat with the other end panel.

4 Cut one piece of backing fabric the length and width of the three panels plus 3 cm (1¼ in) for seam allowance.

5 Place the table runner front right sides together with the backing fabric, with raw edges aligned and pin in place. Stitch one short end of the runner.

6 Now stitch one long edge of the runner. Turn the runner over and stitch the other long edge so that the stitching is running in the same direction on each side, which will reduce puckering.

7 Stitch across the other short end, leaving a gap just big enough to turn the runner through to the right side. Use a blunt object to tease out the corners.

8 Press all the seams flat. Slipstitch the opening closed.

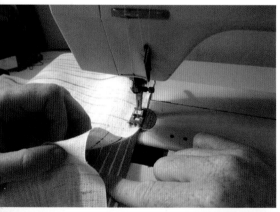

Fabric Baskets

These baskets are very versatile. They can be used to hold bread rolls for an al fresco lunch, to tidy the kids' socks, to hold a pot plant, or even for toys. For this project I have used the masking tape- and bubble wrap-printing techniques. If you are making a set of baskets consider using different print techniques for each, but keep the paint colour the same or similar. The outer hessian (burlap) fabric shown in the photo has been sourced from a recycle shop that sells coffee bean hessian bags with great printed graphics on the outside.

You will need

Scissors
Hessian (burlap)
Tape measure
Masking tape-printed fabric
Sewing machine
Sewing thread
Iron and ironing board

1 Cut a panel of hessian 63 x 23 cm (25 x 9 in). Cut the same from printed fabric for the lining. On each long edge, place a pin 21.5 cm (8½ in) from the corner (four in total). These points will be the corners of the basket.

2 Cut two squares of hessian 23 x 23 cm (9 x 9 in) for two bag sides. Cut the same from printed fabric for the lining.

3 Pin the printed panel around three sides of one printed square, making sure that the corners align with the pins. Clip the corner of the long panel to make it easier to stitch around the corner when sewing.

4 Repeat with the other square printed panel on the other side of the long panel to make an open box shape. Pin and stitch in place. Repeat the last two steps with the hessian outer.

5 Insert the printed fabric basket inside the hessian basket so that right sides are together and raw edges aligned. Stitch around the raw edge joining the outer basket with the printed lining and leave a small gap for turning right side out. Trim the edges, turn right side out, then slip stitch the gap closed.

6 Press and turn a printed lining cuff to the outside.

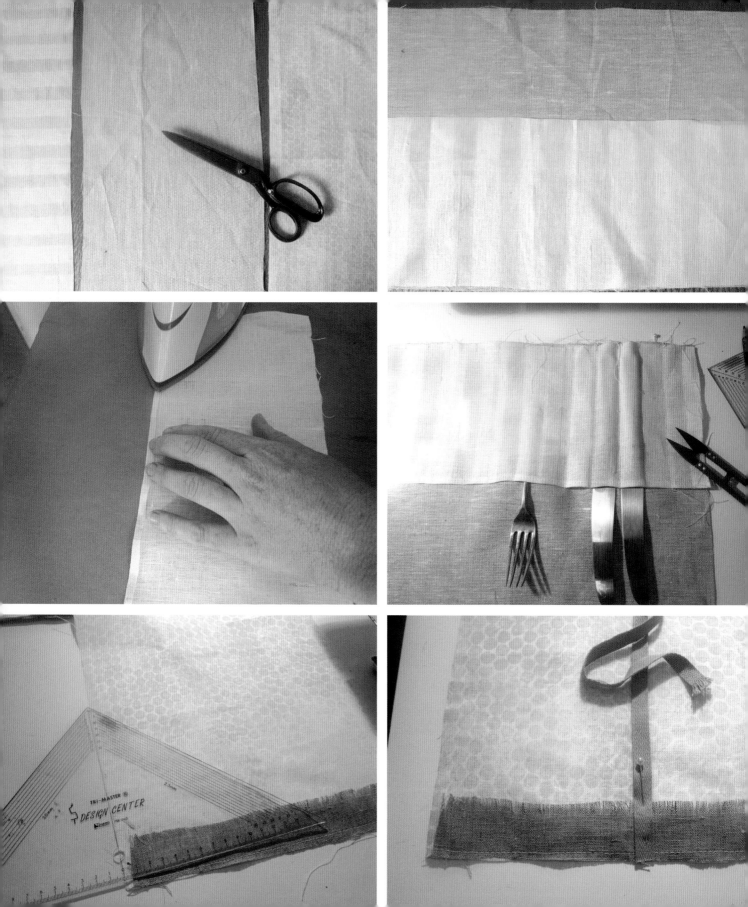

Cutlery Roll

Use this versatile roll to store anything from paintbrushes to crochet hooks. I keep one in my picnic hamper ready to use. I have used fabric printed using two different techniques for this project.

1 Press the fabrics with an iron to remove any creases. From the bubble wrap-printed fabric cut one piece 46 x 27 cm (18¼ x 10½ in). Cut a piece the same size from the plain fabric.

2 For the pocket, from the masking tape-printed fabric, cut one piece 46 cm x 16 cm (18¼ x 6¼ in). Turn under 0.5 cm (¼ in) along one long edge and press. Turn in another 0.5 cm (¼ in) and press. Stitch the pressed hem to form the top edge of the pocket opening using matching thread.

3 With wrong sides together pin the pocket to the lining, aligning one long raw edge. Mark the position of the individual pockets for the cutlery – six for knives and six for forks. The width of each will be determined by the width of your knife and fork handles.

4 Stitch the channels and reinforce the stitching at the top of each pocket for strength.

5 Place the fringed trim or braid onto one short end of the outer panel, aligning the edges and pin in place. Stitch into place at 0.5 cm (¼ in) from the edge. Pin one length of ribbon into the middle of the side that has the fringing and stitch in place. Place the second ribbon onto the outer piece, centred and in 16 cm (6¼ in) from the seam edge. Fold the end over and stitch to hold in place. Top-stitch.

6 Stitch the two panels outer sides together, making sure the ribbons are not caught in the stitching. Stitch around the outside edge, leaving a small opening to turn through. Clip the corners, turn right side out and slip stitch the opening.

Bubble wrap-printed fabric
Iron and ironing board
Plain fabric, for the lining
Masking tape-printed fabric
Tape measure
Fabric scissors
Sewing machine
Matching sewing thread
Air-soluble fabric marker
Pins
Fringed trim or braid, 25 cm (12 in) long (optional)
2 x ribbons, 1 x 35 cm (⅜ x 14 in) long

Lampshade with Fringed Embellishment

You will need

Hot glue gun

Glue sticks

Woven fabric (measure the
   circumference of the drum shade
   and add 4 cm (1½ in) to the
   measurement x the width of the fabric

Tape measure

Fabric marker

Scissors

Drum lightshade (the same diameter at
   the top and bottom)

Fabric scissors

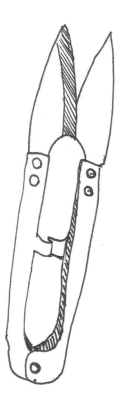

Two different fabrics create subtle texture and an interesting finish on this shade. This is a great lampshade to hang in an entrance or hallway.

1 Cut 5 cm (2 in) wide strips of fabric that are long enough to wrap around the lampshade.

2 To create fringing, carefully tease out threads from one long side of each strip to make a 0.5 cm (¼ in) or longer fringe.

3 Using the tape measure and fabric marker, mark a line every 4 cm (1½ in) around the shade as a guide for gluing.

4 Position the first fabric strip at the bottom edge of the shade so that the fringe overhangs to soften the lower edge of the shade. Remove the strip then glue two glue lines, one at the top and one at the bottom within the 4 cm (1½ in) line. Only apply a small amount of glue so it doesn't dry.

5 Stick the strip in place. To finish each strip, glue the end so it overlaps at the join. Continue gluing and sticking strips until you reach the top.

6 To finish the top edge, cut a fabric strip 3.5 cm (1¼ in) wide and fringe one long edge, as before. Stick the fringed edge in place. Wrap the rest of the strip over the top of the frame to bind it and glue in place. Fold the fabric end and glue in place.

Living

Plain and Printed Cushion Cover

You will need

Iron and ironing board
Fabric scissors
Plain fabric, 81 x 53 cm (32 x 21 in)
Toilet roll-printed fabric, 28 x 53 cm
   (11 x 21 in)
Iron and ironing board
Zipper, 30 cm (12 in)
Sewing machine
Thread
Tape measure
Cushion pad, 50 x 50 cm (20 x 20 in)
Pins
Quick unpick

I decorated the fabric for this project using the toilet roll method of printing You can make marks with many everyday things in your home, so use your imagination and do some experimenting and you might be surprised with the results. My base cloth is linen for both the printed and plain panels.

1 Wash the fabrics for the cushion, leave to dry and press flat. Cut one piece of plain fabric and one piece of print fabric for the cushion front, each 28 x 53 cm (11 x 21 in).

2 Cut one cushion back 53 x 53 cm (21 x 21 in).

3 Put the cushion front pieces right sides together and raw edges aligned and stitch along one 53 cm (21 in) edge using a 1.5 cm (5/8 in) seam allowance. Open out and press the seams flat.

4 Put the cushion front and back pieces right sides together and raw edges aligned. Place a pin 10 cm (4 in) from each end of a plain seam to mark the zipper position. Using a regular stitch length, stitch from one corner up to the pin. Change the stitch length to its longest setting and stitch to the next pin (over the zipper position). Change the stitch length back to a regular length and continue stitching to the raw edge. Open the seam and press flat. Reinforce the stitching at the start and end of the zipper position.

5 Centre the zipper right side down over the wrong side of the seam and pin in place. Using a zipper foot on the sewing machine, stitch the zipper into place 1 cm (3/8 in) from the seam line. Unpick the long stitches over the zipper and press flat.

6 Fold the two pieces right sides together and sew the remaining three sides of the cushion together using a 1.5 cm (5/8 in) seam allowance. Open the zipper and pull through to the right side, pushing the corners out. Press and insert the cushion pad.

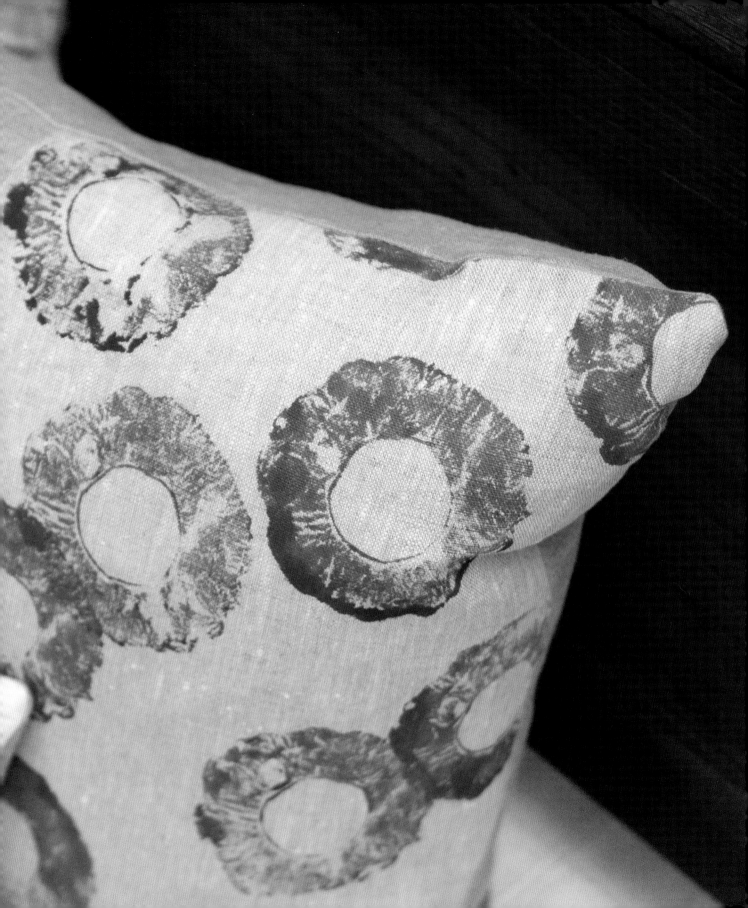

Printed Bolster Cushion

Use a cushion pad that is filled with feathers for this project because you can push them around to fill the cushion effectively. I have used the wooden block printing technique for this project.

1 Wash the fabrics for the cushion, leave to dry and press flat. Cut one piece of printed linen 73 x 53 cm (28¾ x 21 in).

2 Fold in half along the long edge. Pin the long raw edges together, putting a pin 15 cm (6 in) from each end, to mark the zipper position.

3 Stitch the short end at each side of the zipper with a regular stitch length. When you get to the pin, change to the longest stitch (basting stitch), which will be easy to remove, and stitch between the pins. Change back to the shorter stitch when you get to the next pin and sew to the end. Open and press the seams flat.

4 Place the zipper right side down on the wrong side of the seam, centred on the seam line and between the pins. Stitch all around using a zipper foot. Remove the basting stitches with a quick unpick. Open the zipper to test, then close and press flat.

5 Stitch a double row of gathering stitches around each end of the tube. Pull the gathering stitches in as tight as you can. Pleat the gathering in as tightly as possible, then either hand or machine stitch in place depending on the thickness of the fabric. Turn right side out.

6 Using double thread, stitch one covered button over a gathered cushion end to cover any gap in the gathering and to give a neat finish. Press and insert the cushion pad by rolling it to fill.

You will need

Iron and ironing board
Block-printed linen, 80 cm (32 in)
Zipper, 40 cm (16 in)
Sewing machine
Thread
Tape measure
Fabric scissors
Iron and ironing board
Feather cushion inner, 60 x 40 cm
(23¾ x 15¾ in)
Pins
Quick unpick
Sewing needle
2 covered buttons
Length of fringed fabric

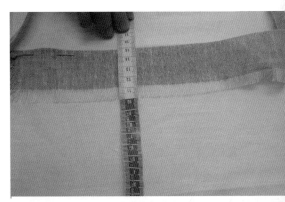

Shibori Square Cushion Cover

I have used a piece of shibori-dyed silk for the front of this cushion and linen for the back. Always cut the fabric larger than the dimensions of the cushion pad in case the fabric shrinks or frays when dyed.

1 Trim the shibori-dyed silk to 53 x 53 cm (21 x 21 in).

2 Cut a piece of backing fabric 53 x 53 cm (21 x 21 in).

3 Place the front and back pieces right sides together and with raw edges aligned. Insert a pin 10 cm (4 in) from each end of the side seam that will contain the zipper. Stitch the seam up to the pin using a regular stitch length, then change to the longest stitch and continue to sew up to the next pin. Change the stitch length back to regular and continue for the rest of the seam. Open the seam and press flat.

4 Place the zipper right side down on the wrong side of the seam and pin in place. Stitch the zipper in place using a zipper foot. Remove the basting stitches and open the side seam so you can open the zip. Reinforce the stitching at each end of the zipper. Press flat.

5 Sew the remaining three sides of the cushion with a 1.5 cm ($^5/_8$ in) seam allowance. Open the zipper and pull through to the right side, pushing the corners out. Press and insert the cushion pad.

Shibori-dyed silk
Fabric scissors
Sewing machine
Backing fabric (linen)
Tape measure
Pins
Thread
Zipper, 30 cm (12 in)
Cushion inner, 50 x 50 cm (20 x 20 in)
Iron and ironing board
Quick unpick

Panel-printed Cushion Cover

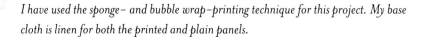

You will need

Iron and ironing board
Bubble wrap-printed fabric
Sponge-printed fabric
Plain linen
Backing fabric
Zipper, 40 cm (16 in)
Pins
Sewing machine
Thread
Tape measure
Scissors
Cushion pad, 60 x 60 cm
    (23½ x 23½ in)
Quick unpick

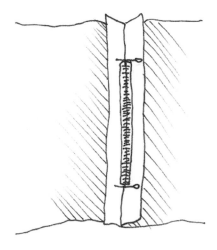

I have used the sponge– and bubble wrap–printing technique for this project. My base cloth is linen for both the printed and plain panels.

1 Wash, dry and press flat the fabrics for the cushion. From bubble wrap-printed fabric, cut one piece 43 x 23 cm (17 x 9 in).

2 From sponge-printed fabric, cut one piece 43 x 43 cm (17 x 17 in).

3 From plain linen, cut one piece 23 x 63 cm (9 x 25 in).

4 From backing fabric, cut one piece 63 x 63 cm (25 x 25 in).

5 Put the sponge-printed panel and bubble wrap-printed panel right sides together aligning the 43 cm (17 in) raw edge. Pin and stitch in place. Open out and press the seam flat.

6 Stitch this printed panel to the plain linen panel along the 63 cm (25 in) edge. Open out and press the seam flat.

7 As an added detail topstitch the panels 1 cm (⅜ in) from the seam line using a complementary coloured thread, if you like. This helps to keep the seams flat and adds strength the stitched panels. Open and press the seams flat.

8 Put the cushion front and back right sides together. Put a pin at 10 cm (4 in) from each end of the side seam where the zipper is to go.

9 Stitch the side of your cushion with a regular length stitch until you reach the first pin (at 10 cm/4 in), then change to the longest stitch and stitch to the next pin. Change back to a regular stitch length and stitch to the corner. Open the seam and press flat.

10 Place the zipper right side down on the wrong side of the seam and pin in place. Stitch the zipper into place 1 cm (⅜ in) from the seam line.

11 Unpick the long stitches covering the zipper and open the zipper. Press flat.

12 Fold the two pieces right sides together and sew the remaining three sides of the cushion using a seam allowance of 1.5 cm (⁵/₈ in).

13 Open the zipper and pull through to the right side, pushing the corners out. Press. Insert the cushion pad.

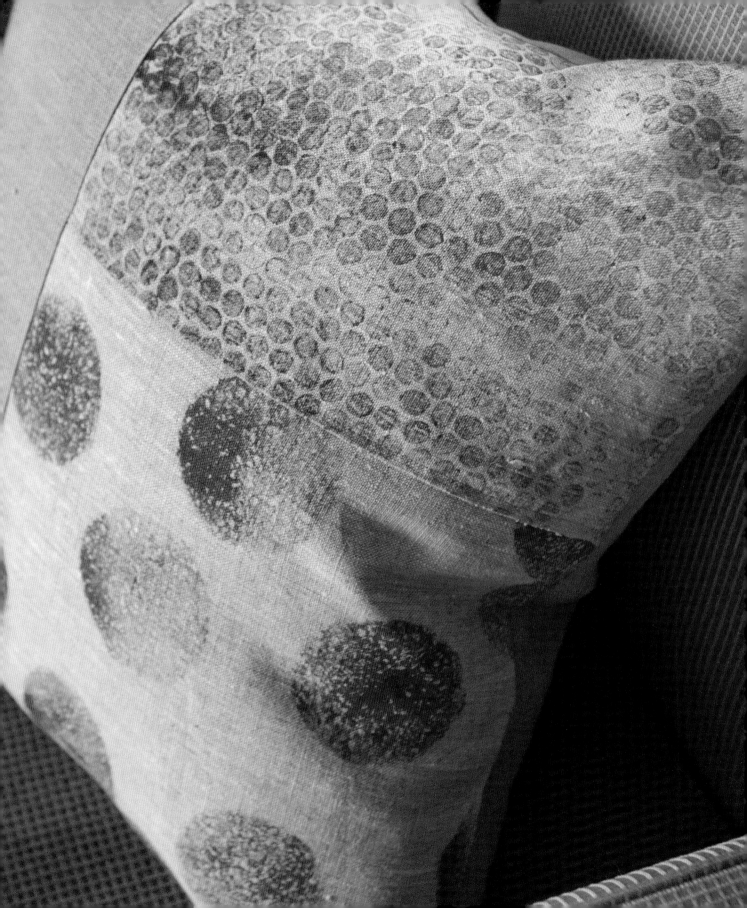

Doorstop

Masking tape-printed fabric,
    50 x 25 cm (18 x 9 in)
Sewing machine
Matching thread
1 x fabric-covered button
Ribbon, 18 cm (7 in)
Rice, 1.5 kg (3½ lb), to fill
Dried lavender flowers
Sewing needle
Wadding (batting)

I have designed this doorstop so that you can make it to any dimensions. During winter when you're not using it to keep the door open, stack these doorstops together for a stylish interior decoration.

1 Fold the printed fabric fabric in half, right sides together and stitch the short edges together to form a tube. Reinforce the beginning and end of the stitching with a reverse stitch.

2 Work one row of gathering stitches 1 cm (¼ in) and another 1.5 cm (½ in) from each raw edge of the tube.

3 Draw up the gathering threads at one end to close the opening. Use a needle and thread to secure the gathered fabric by making a number of stitches.

4 Stitch the fabric-covered button over the gathered centre to hide the stitches.

5 Cut a piece of wadding to the the diameter of the tube and fit in place inside the tube over the gathered end. Fill with rice, then add some dried lavender flowerheads to the mix. Once you have filled the bag two-thirds full, add another circle of wadding on top.

6 Draw up the gathering threads at the other raw edge and stitch securely in place.

7 Fold the ribbon in half and stitch in place over the central gathered area.

Door Snake

Masking tape-printed fabric
Fabric scissors
Tape measure
12 cm (5 in) trim or ribbon,
    2 cm (¾ in) wide
Thread
Iron and ironing board
Sewing machine
Velcro
Pins
Rice, to fill
Dried lavender flowerheads

If you have an old house you'll need lots of these! Draught excluders are easy to make and keep the cold air and critters out in the winter and the hot air out in the summer. I have used the masking tape-method and only printed two-thirds of the fabric.

1 Measure the width of the door. Cut a strip of fabric to that measurement plus 3 cm (1¼ in) for seam allowances x 20 cm (8 in) wide.

2 Fold your fabric in half widthways and notch or mark the centre point of one short edge as a guide to positioning the Velcro.

3 Turn in a 3 cm (1¼ in) hem on the notched edge and press. Place the hook side of the Velcro on one side of the notched pressed edge and the loop half to the other side leaving a 0.5 cm ($^1/_5$ in) gap between the pieces. Stitch in place.

4 On the right side of the fabric, pin the ribbon or trim so that it overlaps the Velcro on the turned edge beneath when folded. Stitch into place using matching thread.

5 Fold the door snake in half and stitch across the bottom and up the side. Pull the snake through to the right side.

6 Fill with rice and the dried lavender flowerheads, which will keep the bugs away and close the Velcro opening.

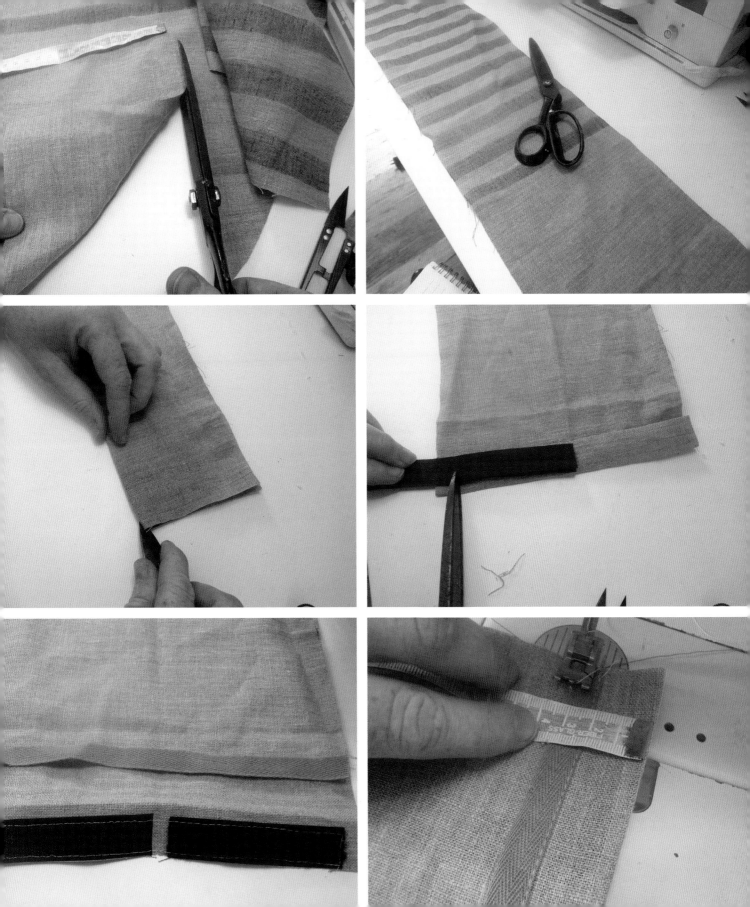

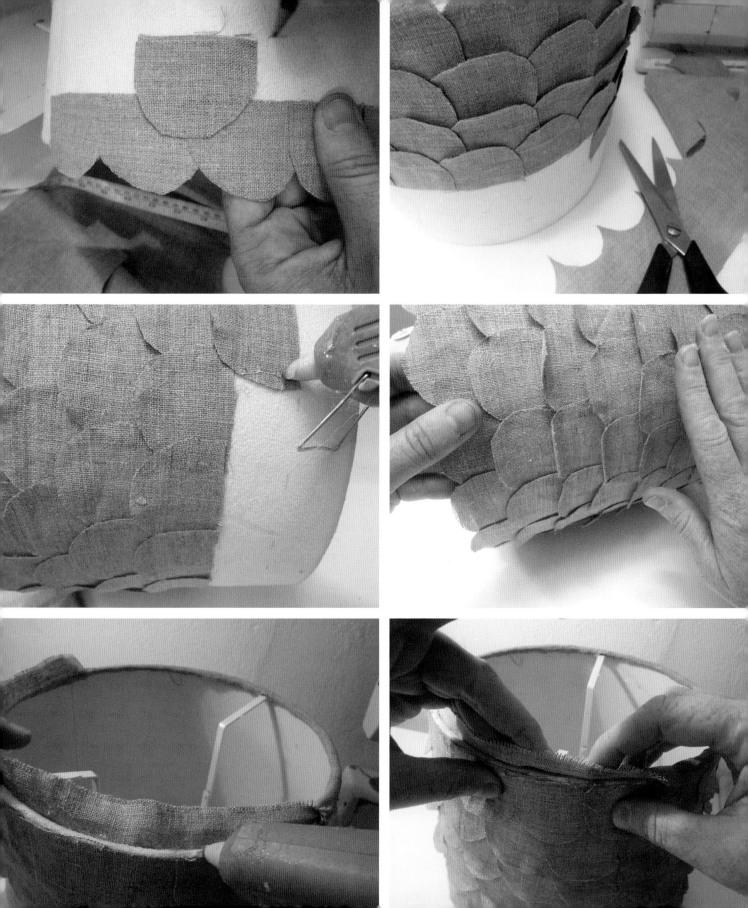

Petal-embellished Lampshade

Give a new lease of life to an old lampshade with this impressive new petal covering. Use offcuts of your favourite fabrics and mix and match the tones for a funky look, or keep it simple and use a single fabric with a soft tonal value.

1 Remove any binding or trim on the lampshade so that you have a smooth, even surface to work on.

2 Trace the template provided for the petal shape. Transfer the tracing to thin card and cut out.

3 Trace around the petal template onto fabric and cut out on the grain. You may need a large number of petals so trace plenty and then cut them out in batches.

4 Place a linen petal on the bottom edge of the lampshade so that it overhangs to create a scalloped edge.

5 Use the template to mark the top edge of the petal all around the lampshade so that you have a guideline to work with to stick the other petals in place. The distance from the bottom of the lampshade to the first line will be repeated up the lampshade to guide you when gluing each line of petals.

6 Heat the glue gun and start gluing the top part of the petals only in place around the bottom edge of the lampshade on the marked line. The unglued petals will curl and give the shade texture. Overlap each petal so you don't see any of the lampshade underneath. It is important to repeat this as evenly as possible. When you switch on the lamp you will see the overlap, which then becomes a textural feature.

You will need

Lampshade
Tracing paper, pencil and thin card
Paper scissors
Linen fabric
Fabric scissors
Fabric marker
Hot glue gun
Glue sticks
Tape measure

7 Continue up to the top of the lampshade working in rounds and positioning each row of petals at even intervals from the last row.

8 Measure the circumference of the top of the lampshade. Cut a strip of linen 2.5 cm (1 in) wide x the circumference plus 1 cm (³/8 in).

9 Remove four of five threads from one long edge of the fabric strip to fray it slightly.

10 Glue the solid edge of the fabric strip from the join line on the lampshade. Glue the inside edge of the lampshade first, tucking in the fabric strip as you go. Apply small amounts of glue as it is easier to manage and the glue will not set.

11 Pull the fabric strip over the top edge of the shade and glue into place on the outside edge.

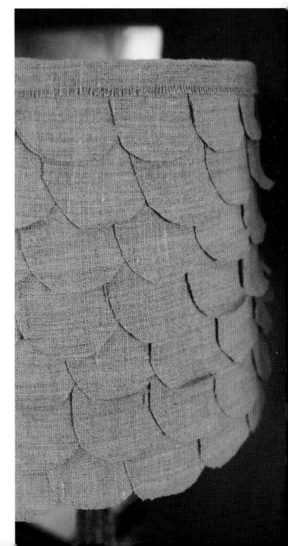

Printed Lampshade

This is a great way of upcycling a tired lampshade and giving it a new lease of life. I used linen as my base cloth and the sponge-printing technique. I checked the look of the fabric for the lampshade with a light shining behind it before cutting it to ensure it created an effect that I like. I have mixed a colour that complements my interior.

1 To make a lampshade pattern, arrange the paper for the pattern on a flat surface. Align the seam of the lampshade so that it is parallel with a straight edge of the paper. Draw along the top and bottom edge of the lampshade while you roll the lampshade along the paper. Stop when you have rotated the lampshade fully. Add 2 cm (¾ in) to one end for the seam to overlap.

2 Arrange the printed fabric on a clean work surface and place the pattern on top. Cut out the fabric using the pattern and adding 2 cm (¾ in) to the top and bottom so the fabric can be rolled over the frame and glued into place.

3 Put a spot of glue at the top of the seamline, then run a very fine line of hot glue down the seam. Place one edge of the printed fabric on the glue line. Be careful not to pull or stretch the fabric. Ensure that the seam allowance protrudes at the top and bottom edges.

4 Moving around the top and the bottom of the shade, add small amounts of glue and stick the fabric in place.

5 When you get to the end, fold over the raw edge of fabric to create a neat edge and glue into place.

6 Turn the top and bottom seam allowances in and glue in place. Trim any loose threads.

Lampshade
Paper, to make a pattern
Pencil and scissors
Printed fabric
Fabric scissors
Hot glue gun
Glue sticks

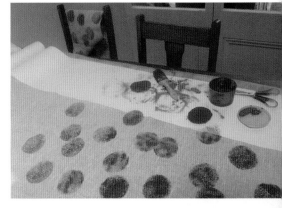

Crocheted Doily Pictures

Iron and ironing board
Picture frames, a selection of the same
    colour
Fabric marker
Linen fabric, for backing
Spray glue
Fabric scissors
Assorted doilies, all the same colour
Double-sided sticky tape

I love the idea of using something handcrafted and from a bygone era in my work. This project offers a perfect opportunity to upcycle handmade crocheted doilies and create a wall decoration for very little cost. We all have some doilies languishing in the linen cupboard waiting for their time to shine. For this project I collected half a dozen and they are all roughly the same size, but with different design details to add interest to the finished artwork.

1 Press the fabric to remove any creases. Remove the back plates from the picture frames and use each as a template to draw around onto the linen backing fabric. Cut out and stick in place using spray glue. The fabric edges will be concealed by the frame.

2 Clean the glass from the picture frames.

3 Place the glass on the work surface. Centre a doily on top, then cover with the covered backing plate. Arrange in a group of five or six on a wall.

bedroom

Button-embellished Pillowcase

Round object, 5 cm (2 in) in diameter
Fabric marker
Pillowcases, in a plain colour
Contrast linen fabric
Scissors
Sewing thread and needle
Assortment of flat, thin buttons

These is a really simply way of transforming pillowcases. Circles of fabric are cut from woven linen and stitched in place along the pillowcase edge. Mother-of-pearl buttons finish the look.

1 Using the round object and fabric marker, draw five to seven circles on the contrast fabric for each pillow, depending on the size of the pillowcase.

2 Cut out the circles and fray the edges by teasing out the horizontal threads.

3 Pin the circles to the opening side of the pillowcase away from where your head will lay. Arrange them so there is an even flow of motifs across the fabric.

4 Centre a button on a fabric circle and stitch in place through the circle and pillowcase. Repeat for the remaining circles.

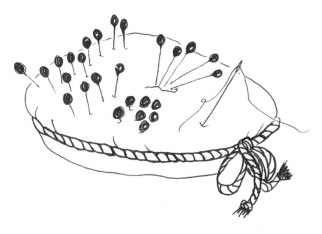

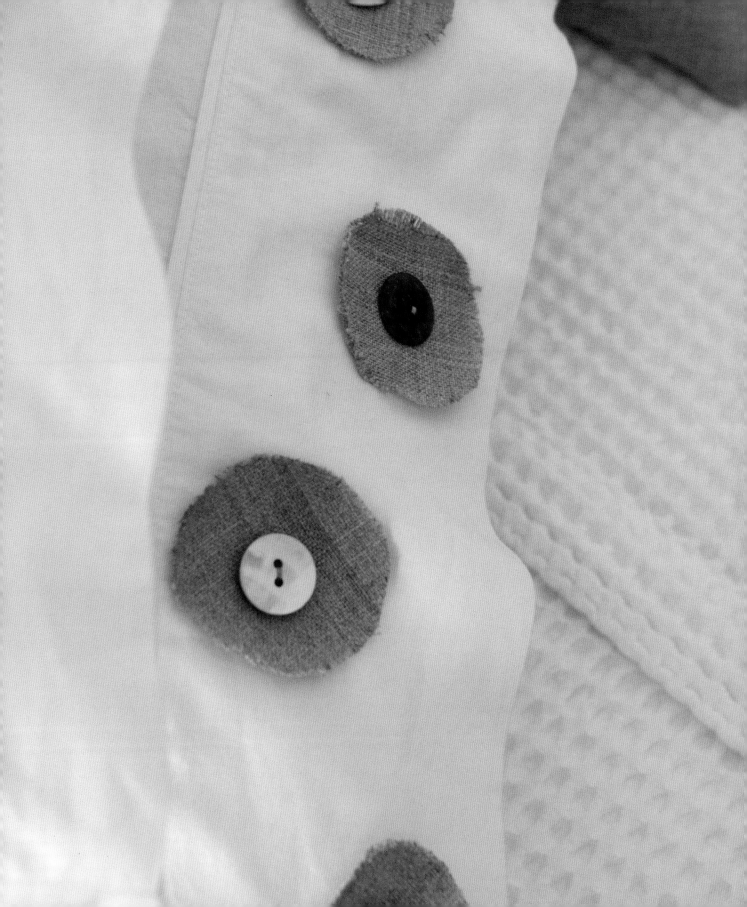

Linen Circles and Ric-rac Braid Pillowcase

You will need

Egg cup
Fabric marker
Pillowcases, in a plain colour
Fabric
Fabric scissors
Ric-rac braid
Sewing machine
Sewing thread
Iron and ironing board

Half circles of cool linen form a decorative pillowcase edging. The raw edges are concealed by ric-rac braid.

1 Draw around the base of an egg cup on plain paper. Cut out the circle. Trim off one side so that you are left with slightly more than a half circle. Use this as your template to cut out enough pieces of fabric to fit across the width of the pillowcase.

2 Pin the half circles in place in a neat line across the opening side of the pillowcase, 8 cm (3¼ in) in from the edge. Baste in place. Pin ric-rac braid over the top of the straight raw edge of the circles.

3 Open both side seams of the pillowcase just enough to poke the ric-rac braid through, then stitch closed. Topstitch the ric-rac braid in place, catching the fabric half circles into the stitching. Press with an iron.

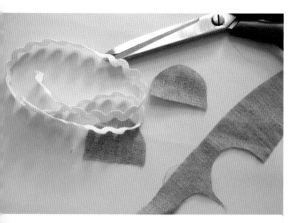

Fringed and Trimmed Pillowcase

A simple strip of textured linen is frayed along one edge and stitched to a plain pillowcase edging. The raw edge is concealed under contrast ric-rac braid.

1 Cut a piece of linen fabric the width of the pillowcase plus 3 cm (1¼ in) x 5 cm (2 in) wide.

2 Gently tease out the threads from one long edge to create a 1 cm (⅜ in) fringed edge with a pin, sewing needle or the point of clippers.

3 Open both side seams of the pillowcase, just wide enough to poke the fringe through.

4 Pin the fringe across the opening side of the pillowcase, 8 cm (3¼ in) in from the edge. Baste in place.

5 Pin the braid on top of the long raw edge of the fringed fabric and stitch in place.

6 Poke the fringe and braid through the openings at both ends. Turn the pillowcase inside out and stitch the opening closed, catching the fringing and braid in the stitching.

Fabric scissors
Linen fabric
Tape measure
Pillowcases, in a plain colour
Pins
Braid, ribbon or lace
Sewing thread
Sewing machine

Embellished Cushion

This is a cushion that has decorated my bed for years and every so often I decide to change the look. So, I think this is cushion cover number... 4!

1 Measure the cushion pad. Add 3 cm (1¼ in) to the length and width for seam allowances and cut two pieces of fabric to your measurement for the cushion front and back.

2 Cut six strips of the contrast fabric 5.5 (2¼ in) x the length of the cushion cover. Create a 1 cm (⅜ in) fringe on one long edge of each strip by carefully teasing out and discarding the horizontal threads.

3 Turn in and press 0.5 cm (¼ in) along one long edge of each strip.

4 On the cushion front, measure and mark even intervals across the width. This will be where you place each fringed strip.

5 Pin the strips in place and stitch 2 mm (⅛ in) from the folded edge. Press with an iron.

6 Put the cushion front and back right sides together. Put a pin 10 cm (4 in) from each end of one side seam to mark the zipper position.

Cushion pad
Tape measure
Fabric , to cover your chosen cushion
Fabric, with a different
colour and texture for decoration
Iron and ironing board
Zipper, 40 cm (16 in)
Iron and ironing board
Sewing machine
Thread
5.5 cm (2¼ in) of fringing,
1 cm (⅜ in) wide
Embroidery thread

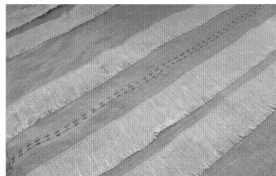

7 Stitch the side seam with a regular stitch length until you reach the first pin, then change to a longer stitch until you reach the next pin. Return to the shorter stitch length from the second pin to the raw edge. Open the seam and press flat.

8 Place the zipper right side down on the wrong side of the seam and pin in place. Stitch the zipper in position using a zipper foot. Reinforce the stitching at each end of the zipper. Unpick the basting stitches to open the side seam so you can open the zipper. Press flat.

9 Fold the two cushion halves right sides together and sew the remaining three sides of the cushion with a 1.5 cm (⁵/₈ in) seam allowance. Open the zipper and pull through to the right side, pushing the corners out. Insert the cushion pad.

Covered Coathanger

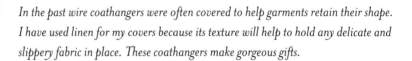

You will need

Wire coathangers
Tape measure
Linen fabric
Iron and ironing board
Sewing machine
Thread
Fabric scissors
Hot glue gun
Glue stick
Braid/trim/fringe
String or ribbon

In the past wire coathangers were often covered to help garments retain their shape. I have used linen for my covers because its texture will help to hold any delicate and slippery fabric in place. These coathangers make gorgeous gifts.

1 Put the coathanger on the wrong side of the linen and draw around the outer edge. Draw a straight line across connecting the two points at each side of the neck of the hook. Add 2 cm (¾ in) to the bottom straight edge of the coathanger. Add 1.5 cm (⅝ in) all around for seam allowances.

2 Cut two pieces of linen for each hanger.

3 Turn in and press 1 cm (⅜ in) at the point where the hook will feed through the top of each cover. Press and stitch. The smaller the opening the neater it will look.

4 Place the two sides of the hanger cover right sides together and stitch the shoulders together. Turn right side out and press.

5 Turn in a small hem around the opening of the cover and press.

6 Arrange the braid/trim/fringe along the bottom edge and topstitch in place, catching down the hem at the same time.

7 Cut a strip of linen 1 x 20 cm (³/8 x 8 in). Add a dab of hot glue to the tip of the hook and stick the end of the linen strip to it. Wind the linen around the hook to cover it. Glue to secure the other end of the linen strip in place.

8 Add a piece of string or ribbon to the neck of the hook to finish.

Embellished Curtains

You will need

Pair of curtains
Fabric (that co-ordinates with your
    curtain)
Round object 6 cm (2½ in) diameter
Fabric marker
Fabric scissors
Iron and ironing board
Pins
Curtains
Thread
Embroidery thread

Small circles of linen are stitched at random over the curtains. They are each then decorated with neat embroidery stitches.

1 On the right side of the fabric, draw about 20 circles for each curtain, each 6 cm (2½ in) diameter, using a round object as a template, for example, an egg cup. Cut out the circles and press them.

2 Fray the edges of each circle to give texture and dimension.

3 Pin your circles to the curtain, arranging them so there is an even flow of motifs on the fabric. Place the circles close together at the base and more widely spaced as you work up the curtain.

4 Hand stitch the circles in place with embroidery thread, mixing the styles with, for example, a criss-cross stitch, double circles, large stitches or small stitches. Press and hang the curtains.

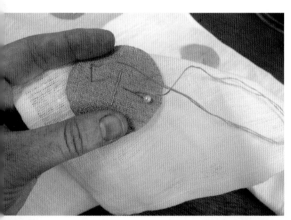

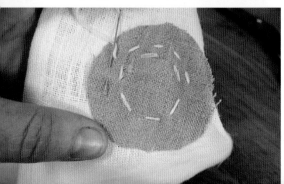

Wheat Bag

What could be better after a long day, than sitting with a heat pack behind your back or resting behind your neck? Just a minute in the microwave is all it takes to transform this wheat bag into a contemporary version of a hot water bottle, complete with lavender scent. Make sure you check the temperature before use so its not too hot. I used the Japanese shibori dyeing technique for this project.

1 Cut one piece of shibori-dyed silk and one piece of linen 49 x 17 cm (19¼ x 7 in). Place right sides together and sew around the edges using a 1.5 cm (½ in) seam and leaving an opening to fill with the grain and herbs.

2 Fill with your choice of grain and herbs, but don't overstuff the bag — it should mould easily to your body and not be too heavy.

3 Slip stitch the opening closed using a needle and thread or use your sewing machine.

Shibori-dyed silk
Linen, for backing
Fabric scissors
Matching thread
Sewing machine
Rice, barley, wheat or corn, to fill
20 ml (4 tsp) lavender, rosemary or cloves
Sewing needle

lifestyle

Journal Cover

Iron and ironing board
Printed linen, to fit the dimensions of
    your book plus 4 cm (1½ in) extra
    all around
Fabric scissors
Black ribbon or twill tape, to wrap
    around the book
Journal with hard cover
Contrast linen
Matching thread
Sewing machine
Sewing needle
Ruler or tape measure

I like to carry a journal in which I can note my thoughts and visual inspiration, so I have created a removable cover to make it special. My grandmother Adrianne always covered her books in beautiful floral linens left over from upholstering or soft furnishing and she inspired this project. I used the paper doily-printing method. Use the same colour palette to co-ordinate all your book covers for an interesting display on your bookshelf.

1 Iron the printed fabric to remove all creases.

2 Cut the ribbon to wrap around the width of the book plus at least 12 cm (5 in) extra to tie the cover closed, depending on the thickness of the book.

3 To make the fringing, cut a 4 cm (1½ in) wide strip of linen long enough to wrap around the width of the book. Use a contrast fabric, if you like. Pull and remove 4 or 5 threads from around all edges to create a fringed effect. Leave the rest of the ribbon free to use to tie the book closed.

4 Centre the fringing across the width of the linen. Put the ribbon on top and pin in place. Sew the fringing-covered ribbon to the linen background by hand or machine using matching thread. If you decide to hand sew, consider using an embroidery thread and running stitch. Press. Leave the rest of the ribbon free to tie the book closed.'

5 Stitch around the entire piece of fabric turning the edge in 2 mm (⅛ in) and stitch. Trim all loose threads and press.

6 Place the cover inside out on the book and turn the flaps over the side of book cover and pin the cover. Remove to stitch the flaps, which hold the cover in place. Reverse stitch at the beginning and end to strengthen the cover. Turn the corners out and press.

Shibori Scarf

You will need

Scarf or length of silk to a scarf length
Iron and ironing board
Clothes pegs (pins)
Liquid dye
3 buckets
Dye fixative
Newspaper
Sewing machine
Thread
Sewing needle
Scissors
Braid (optional)

The challenge with this technique is to try and create a design with some regularity in the pattern. I cut my fabric to the desired scarf dimensions before I dyed it in order to manipulate the shibori dye pattern successfully.

1 Concertina fold the scarf. Press each fold with an iron and hold in place with clothes pegs. If the scarf is wider than the pegs, fold the scarf in half widthwise after completing the folding.

2 Mix the dye in a bucket according to the manufacturer's instructions. Fill another bucket with cold water for rinsing. Mix the dye fixative in another bucket according to the manufacturer's instructions.

3 Dip the folded edge of the scarf in dye (the resulting stripe will be twice as wide as the dip).

4 Dip the folded edge in the bucket of cold water to rinse it.

5 Dip the folded edge in fixative to set the colour.

6 Clip the folded scarf to a clothes line. Place newspaper beneath the scarf to collect any drips. Leave until completely dry, about one day. Unfold the scarf and press with an iron.

7 Cut the length of silk into two pieces each 33 cm (13 in) wide. Place the lengths right sides together and raw edges aligned. Pin, then stitch all the way around leaving a small opening to turn right side out.

8 Turn the scarf right side out and tease out the corners. Press with an iron and slipstitch the opening closed. If your fabric is very lightweight you may want to sew a trim or braid to each end to give it more weight.

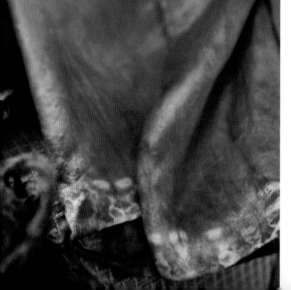

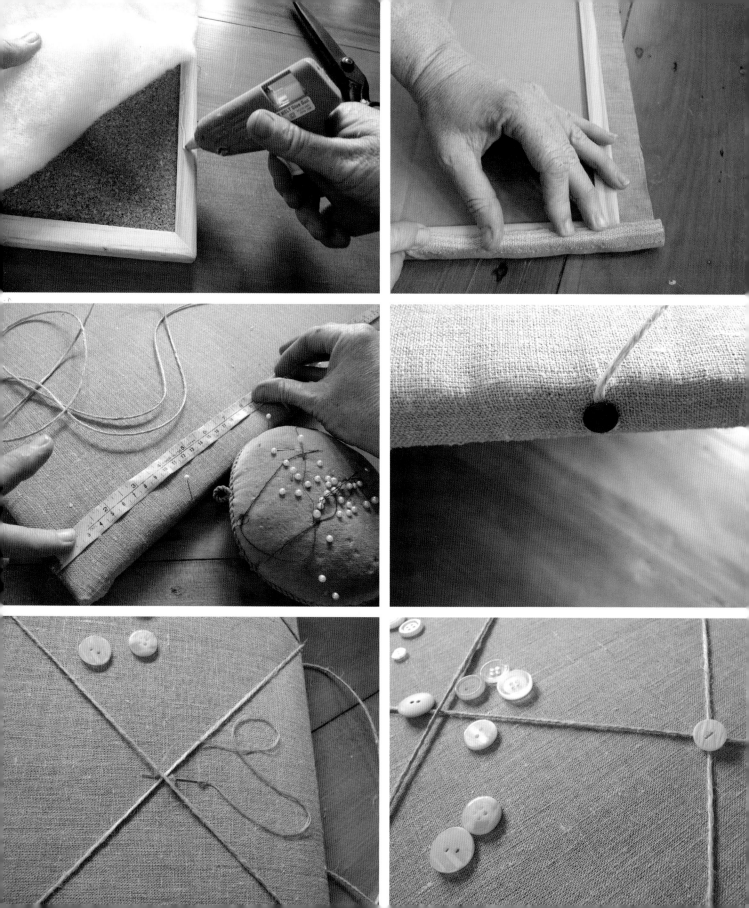

Fabric Noticeboard

I love to use my noticeboard as a mood board on which I pin inspiration for my designs from my travels. Swatches of fabric, postcards, photos, threads, trims and buttons will all appear at different times.

1 Cut the wadding to fit the dimensions of the cork board exactly with no overhang.

2 Stick the wadding to the outer edge of the cork board using the hot glue gun.

3 Iron the fabric to remove any creases. Using fabric scissors, cut the fabric slightly larger than the surface of the corkboard so that there is enough fabric to wrap around the outer edge of the board.

Place the fabric right side down on the work surface. Put the cork board, wadding side down on top. Apply glue to the top edge of the cork board frame and stick the fabric in place, making sure that you pull the fabric taut and it has an even tension over the frame.

5 Glue the opposite edge of the board and stick the fabric in place, again pulling it so that it is taut with an even tension. Secure a small area at a time so the glue doesn't set before the fabric is fastened.

6 At the corners fold the fabric neatly in the same way as you would a hospital corner when making a bed. Glue as you go, securing each fold with pins until dry. Leave to dry.

7 The string or ribbon is fastened across the front of the fabric in a diamond grid design. Measure and mark with pins at intervals along each edge of the board, making sure that the markings are exactly opposite.

8 Tie one end of the string to a tack and insert the tack on the edge of the board at the first mark from the corner. Then wind the string across the board to the diagonally opposite marker. Tack in place. Repeat at each mark.

9 When you work in the opposite sides, weave the string over and under the strings it crosses. Once you have finished attaching your string, secure it at the side with tacks.

10 With a needle and thread, stitch the intersections to the fabric cover. Then stitch an assortment of similarly coloured buttons over the intersections.

11 Attach your noticeboard to the wall using Velcro.

Shower Cap

I have used the paper doily-printing technique for this project.

1 From the plastic cut one circle, 48 cm (19 in) in diameter. Cut the same from the printed fabric.

2 Put the plastic circle on top of the right side of the printed fabric and stitch together 0.2 cm (⅛ in) from the raw edges.

3 To make the casing for the elastic, press open one side of the wider binding. Align the opened-out edge of the binding with the raw edge of the underside of the cap and pin in place. Stitch the binding in place along both sides, but leave the join open to thread the elastic through.

4 Open out one side of the narrow binding and pin, then stitch in place aligning the edge with the raw edges of the underside of the cap. Fold the binding over to the right side of the cap and pin, then topstitch in place.

5 Using a safety pin, thread the elastic through the casing. Stitch both ends together, then slipstitch the opening in the binding closed.

You will need

Soft pliable plastic, for the cap
Printed fabric
Scissors
Tape measure
Sewing machine
Thread
Bias binding, 3 cm (1¼ in) wide
Bias binding, 1.2 cm (½ in) wide
Elastic
Safety pin

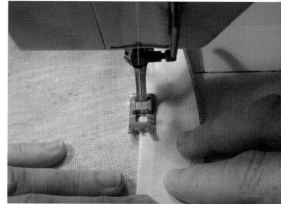

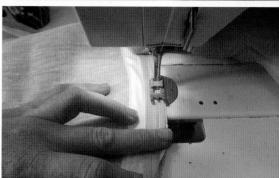

Fabric Flowers

You will need

Vintage fabrics remnants
Fabric scissors
Hot glue gun
Glue sticks
Hair clips, brooch pin, hat, head band
    (optional)
6 pieces of string, 7 cm (3 in) long
Fabric-covered button and threads

These flowers are fun and easy to make and have so many uses. Use them to accessorise hats or even lamps, stitch to a brooch pin or hair slide to make a statement piece of jewellery, or use as a lavish gift wrap trimming.

1 Cut 6 circles from fabric remnants. The circles that I cut were each 4 cm (1¾ in) diameter.

2 If the fabric is woven, tease out the strands of cloth to fray the edges.

3 Arrange the petal circles into one large circle so that the edges overlap.

4 Cut a 2 cm (¾ in) square of fabric and glue to the centre back of the circle to hold the petals together. Leave to dry. Glue a hair clip or brooch pin to the fabric square and leave to dry.

5 To make the tufted flower centres, hold string lengths together and fold in half. Tease each end with your fingers to unravel the thread slightly. Use hot glue to stick the tufts to the centre of the flower. Alternatively, sew a fabric-covered button in the centre.

Tote Bag

You will need

Sponge-printed/bubble wrap-printed
     fabric
Tape measure
Scissors
Calico, for lining
Bubble wrap-printed fabric
Pins
Sewing machine
Matching thread
Needle
Heavy bead
Tape measure
Ribbon or thick tape, 110 x 4 cm
     (43½ x 1¾ in)
Sewing needle

This is a simple and funky bag, which is easy to make. I have used a combination of sponge– and bubble wrap–printing on linen, using both techniques on the one piece of fabric. Use the fold line on the template as your defining line. The bubble wrap print is on the back of the bag and the flap, and the sponge circles are on the front. You can use a piece of masking tape to create a clean fold line defining the two prints.

1 Cut one piece of your sponge-printed/bubble wrap-printed fabric using the Tote Bag template.

2 From calico, cut one piece of fabric for the lining using the Tote Bag template.

3 With right sides of the printed fabric together and raw edges aligned, pin and then stitch the bag front and bag back together around the two sides. Turn right side out. Stitch the calico front and back lining together in the same way, leaving a gap in one side seam of the lining through which the finished bag will be turned right side out.

4 Insert the printed bag inside the lining so that right sides are together and raw edges align. Pin the lining to the printed bag around the top raw edges. Pin the flaps together. Stitch in place. Turn right side out through the gap. Slip stitch the gap closed.

5 Tease out the lower point of the flap. Stitch a heavy bead on the point to provide weight and help the bag stay closed.

6 To make the strap, turn in the raw edges at each end of the ribbon or thick tape. Pin in place over the side seams 4 cm (1¾ in) beneath the top edge of the bag. Stitch the folded edge, diagonally across the tape for strength and then across the top, reverse stitching at the beginning and the end to reinforce.

Christmas Decoration

Craft knife and self-healing cutting mat
Stencil plastic
Hessian (burlap)
Fabric paint
Paint brush with thick bristles
Scissors
Sewing machine
String, cut into 25 cm (10 in) lengths

This is an easy decoration to make and will give your tree a homespun look. Make them in lots of shapes, but keep the colour scheme festive. They look great en masse on the Christmas tree or hanging from the window.

1 Decide on the shape you want, I have chosen to make a star. You could make a bird or a Christmas tree.

2 Draw your chosen shape in the centre of a piece of stencil plastic. Then cut it out using a craft knife, working on a cutting mat and ensuring the shape has a neat edge.

3 Hold the stencil securely on the hessian. Using fabric paint and a brush, dab or stipple the paint onto the hessian through the stencil.

4 Cut out the stencilled shape, allowing an extra 1 cm ($^3/_8$ in) all around. This will frame the print and be the seam allowance.

5 Cut a plain piece of hessian to back the decoration, or use another printed piece. This will make the shape stiffer.

6 Sandwich your piece of string into one corner between the layers.

7 Place your plain and printed fabric stars wrong side together and stitch with a wide zigzag stitch around the outside using a matching thread. Trim any loose threads.

8 Alternatively, you could sew a button to the centre of the star and loop a length of string around the button to make a napkin ring.

168   lifestyle

Christmas Stocking

These make fabulous handcrafted presents for small children and are sure to become a significant part of a family's Christmas tradition. Personalise each stocking by printing or embroidering the person's initials onto the cuff. I have used the stencil-printing technique to decorate fabric with a star motif. The stars have been cut out and stitched on top of the stocking.

1 Photocopy the templates provided over the page to the required scale. Cut out the templates adding an extra allowance for the folded cuff.

2 Cut two stockings from hessian using the template as a guide. Cut out one toe panel from contrasting linen fabric.

3 Pin the toe panel in place on top of the right side of one hessian stocking. Baste in place. Pin the ric-rac braid over the raw edge of the linen and topstitch in place.

4 Using red fabric paint, print your stars on separate fabric, then cut out and stitch them in the centre onto the stocking.

5 Place the front and back stockings right sides together and stitch around the outside edge leaving the top open. Reverse stitch at the start, end and over the loop to reinforce your sewing. Turn right side out.

6 Turn in a 1 cm (⅜ in) hem at the top raw edge and press. Turn down the cuff and topstitch in place.

7 Fold the hanging ribbon in half. Pin in place on the back of one stocking, aligning raw edges and positioning it just inside the top edge of the stocking.

8 I have added a fringe and ric-rac braid to finish the cuff off. Press.

Hessian (burlap)
Paper scissors
Fabric scissors
Contrasting linen fabric

Sewing thread
Needle
Pins
Ric-rac braid
Sewing machine
Fabric paint
Stencil plastic
Cutting blade
Decorative buttons
Ribbon, for hanging

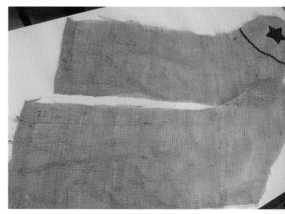

About the Author

Fiona Fagan has a passion for textiles. She trained as a pattern maker and later as a textile designer, using the harsh rural landscape in which she grew up as inspiration for her designs. Fiona learned to sew at a young age and quickly developed an awareness of and interest in beautiful fabrics.

In her career Fiona has designed bed linen, swimwear, fashion, ceramics, soft furnishings and stationery. Her designs encompass traditional hand-painted and computer-generated designs, and always use natural fabrics.

Fiona currently runs Simply This, a small independent textile company based in Sydney, Australia, which specialisies in printing fabrics with interesting design elements and transforming them into items of soft furnishings.

Since 2010, Fiona has been engaged as a visual artist for Moorambilla Voices, a choir group for children, producing hand-dyed costumes, designing the Moorambilla Festival T-shirt and leading workshops with the local community. www.simplythis.com.au

Index